REVEALING THE
obvious

finding the
creative
genius
in your
everyday
life

steve buck

Copyright © 2021 by Elephantine Press, LLC

All rights reserved.
Published in the United Sates by Elephantine Press, LLC, Tampa, FL
www.elephantinepress.org

Elephantine Press books are available at special discount for bulk purchases for educational, sales promotions or corporate use. Special editions, including personalized covers, excerpts of existing books, or books with corporate identity, can be produced in large quantities for specials needs. For information, contact Customer Service at 813.825.2020 or email unique@elephantinepress.org .

Library of Congress Cataloging-in-Publication Data
Buck, Steve.
 Revealing the obvious: finding the creative genius in your everyday life/by Steve Buck - 1st Edition
   p.cm.
 Includes bibliographical index and notes.
 1. Self Help. 2. Business. 3. Management.
 I. Buck, Steve. II. Title
   Library of Congress Control Number: 2021922894

ISBN 979-8-9852619-0-5
eISBN 979-8-9852619-1-2

Printed in the United States of America

Book design by Steve Buck
Cartoons by Phillip Ortiz
Cover Design by Steve Buck
Cover Illustration by Photobank/Adobe Stock

10 9 8 7 6 5 4 3 2

First Edition

In grateful appreciation:

To the source of my transcendent gift of creativity
that has never failed
and never will.

To my loving and infinitely patient wife Keiko who never questioned my long hours
of writing out in the camper with Pooch.

To Stratton Smith who started this whole thing when he called me
"The Master of the Obvious."

introduction i

This is not literature.

It is a workbook. It is not the Great American Novel[1]. It is meant to be written in, used, bent, folded, spindled and mutilated[2]. Highlight it. Tear pages out. Cover it with Post-It's[3]. Fold over the corners. Wear it out.

When I was first becoming aware of having become co-dependent in a specific relationship years ago, I came across a very seminal discourse on co-dependency[4]. The first time I read it, I highlighted a couple of things. The second time, it looked more like a used college textbook. By the time I had read through it three times, practically the entire book glowed neon yellow from all the highlighters I had used up in its interior, and thoroughly wrinkle-warped by all the ballpoint pen notes in the margins. It is my hope you will wear out your copy of this book, as well.

The book is not particularly long. It is not complex. In fact, it's deceptively simple. It can be read in a single (if not protracted) sitting, but not fully absorbed after several readings. I won't put it in the same category as "The Art of War[5]" by Sun Tszu, but it is equally as easy to gloss over – and miss the point. Your call.

I have highlighted obvious focal points in "note form" throughout. They make handy visual references when scanning or re-scanning the book. I have also included an "obvious checklist" at the end of each chapter so you can make sure you saw and/or grasped the key messages in each one. Additionally, I have included numerical keys adjacent to words, idioms or concepts that may not be in your current toolbox. These key references are in the, "What the heck did he just say...?" Section in the back of the book. You can ignore it, reference it when necessary or use it continuously throughout your obvious adventure to find all the little nuggets of wisdom embedded in this simple little book. It is not required reading, but you never know what you might find if you just dig a little deeper.

Finally, for those of us (me included) who really prefer a "book with pictures," I have included "The Obvious Path." It is a cartoon adventure of two unlikely friends named Schnitzl & P'Nut (I'm sure you can figure out which is which.) Schnitzl is a wired (possibly over-caffeinated) little seeker that just can't sit still. Her mouth often works before her brain is engaged. P'Nut, on the other hand, is a lumbering, gentle giant with a slow internal clock speed[6]. But, don't underestimate him. He's very smart. Between the two of them, they wrestle with the concepts of "obviosity[7]" in each chapter. Sometimes they do well, other times, not so much. Kinda' like me.

However you choose to use the book *IS* the right way. There are no wrong ways. Should you end up using it to prop up a wobbly kitchen table, so be it. At least it's functional and serving an obvious purpose. I will consider it a success. Besides, most people don't understand me right away, anyway.

❖

table of contents

chapters

1. The most annoying person you will ever meet .. 1
2. Occam had a Razor 9
3. Oblivious to the Obvious 23
4. "But, I'm not creative." 33
5. Trust is the Key 49
6. Excellence out of Imbalance 65
7. "Cogni...what?" 81
8. Obviously Toxic 97
9. Elephant in the Room 113
10. The Obvious Lifestyle 127
11. "OK, what's the catch?" 141
12. Whatever you do, Be Obvious 155
13. The Obvious Payoff 175
14. Closing Thoughts 181
    "What the heck did he just say...?" 183
    Other stuff 237

chap 1

the most annoying person you will ever meet

True. I am perhaps the most annoying person you will ever meet. But not for the reasons you might expect. Oh, I'm friendly enough. Witty, charming, good-looking, modest (ahem…) and generally likeable. But, I don't tolerate bullies, boors or abuse – verbal or physical. I do not suffer fools lightly. I have a very low B.S. tolerance and lies are totally unacceptable to me. So, in most cases I tend to be uncomfortably outspoken and the really annoying part is (wait for it…)

(wait for it…)

I reveal the obvious truth.

There You have it. And what's the most annoying part of it is: That the vast majority of people already knew, in their hearts, the truth of what I just stated… before I said it. Now this could simply be annoying in the same way as watching TV when some wildly enthusiastic commercial comes on that is selling the exact same invention that *you* thought of years ago. Or it may be simply declaring that "The Emperor is not wearing any clothes![8]" Or it may be revealing the truth that your audience simply didn't want to

annoying

hear. In any event, revealing the obvious is annoying on so many levels, to so many degrees and to so many people that the faint of heart simply avoid it, return their heads to the sand and thereby offer a very unfortunate presentation of themselves to the world at large.

But, it doesn't have to be that way. Speaking the obvious truth can be very liberating for both the speaker and the listener. The obvious truth defends itself. It stands on its own two feet (Assuming, of course, that truth has feet, let alone two of them) But, I digress[9]. You'll find that to be quite obvious as you read through this book. It's even worse in person.

Obviously, there's a right way and a wrong way to reveal the obvious truth. And sadly, sometimes there is no right way. Over the years I have discovered, the hard way, the benefits of presenting the obvious in the best possible fashion. Words can give life, or destroy it. They can encourage or demoralize. They can placate or enrage. It's all in the presentation. For example, there's more than one way to communicate this idea. You could tell someone, "Your face could stop a clock." OR – you could say, "When I gaze into your

the obvious path

face, all time stands still." It's the same message. Just a different delivery. The question becomes, "Is there really any value in making *that* particular statement."

Obviously, no.

But sometimes truths do need to be revealed, whether they are uncomfortable or not. The art is in the presentation. Let the truth be your shield. But, be careful when you poke the bear.[10] He may stop when he sees the truth that you're holding up in front of him, OR - he may perceive it as an existential threat and attack it (and you) with all his force, cunning and skill. There's a difference between being "right" and being "dead right."

Being obvious is not easy, or for the timid. But speaking the truth to power has always been annoying and often very dangerous. This is where wisdom comes into play.

The good news is that wisdom is readily available for the asking. Look around you. As long as there have been people on this planet, there are those purporting to have wisdom and will share it. Either eagerly, or

with a little coaxing. Because wisdom is, in its essence… obvious.

Wisdom is always true. It's always obvious to the sincere seeker. And always benefits the recipient. The trick is in its appropriation and application. Not as easy as it sounds. But, when embraced – in the proper order – wisdom, understanding and knowledge are a potent combination. Especially when applied to creativity. Let's begin.

Wisdom has often been contrasted with experience. Experience has been defined as what happens to *you*. Conversely, wisdom has been defined as somebody else's experience. Wise words, but that's the point. It's obvious.

As human beings, we want to immediately drop right down to the granular level. We want to know the details of application. "What should I do?" "Just give me the details and turn me loose. I'll see you at the top! (and all those other PMA[11] aphorisms.[12])" We want knowledge *now* and have been told for innumerable generations that "knowledge is power." "So, give it to me – NOW!!" In one way that is true, but without having wisdom in place first – *and its understanding* – it leads directly to erroneous conclusions and fallacious, if not downright damaging consequences.

Very bad mojo.

So, wisdom becomes a very watershed[13] bullet in one's bandolier[14] (to mix a metaphor.) If you don't have it in its rightful place, as preeminent among all your other characteristics, you're sadly out of order. I don't mean out of order like eating dessert first (which I highly recommend. Life is short and uncertain), or like a broken parking meter. I mean out of order like locking the barn *after* the horse is stolen. Pretty doggone dumb.

Trophies only count if they yield something permanent

Then, without having the understanding of wisdom, wisdom becomes just another pretty knick-knack on the trophy shelf of your life. As meaningless as that rhodium plated, vinyl clad, wood-grained plastic trophy you won for taking the Intramural (*fill-in-the-blank*) Championship ten years ago. It was important to you and perhaps others at the time, but pretty irrelevant now. Unless of course, you have applied or transferred the skills that got you that trophy, on a regular and on-going basis, in your life or the life of others. (translation: appropriation and application)

But how do you apply or transfer it to the rest of your life? Ah, there you go again. Jumping right to the granular level. "What do I need to do… right now?" And you will have learned nothing. It's like giving someone directions based on right and left turns. As soon as you miss one or there's a detour – you're lost. But if you have a map and an understanding of North/South/East/West, you can still get there. You need to own it.

You must first seek wisdom and then understand it so you can appropriate it into your life. Make it part and parcel of your very being. Make your behavior indistinguishable from the actual wisdom itself. In the words of that great, intergalactic philosopher of long, long ago and far, far away, Yoda[15]: "There is no try, only do." But, there we go back to the granular level, again. "OK. So, how do I gain understanding of wisdom?"

Ahh, *now* we're getting somewhere. That's exactly the right question.

To understand wisdom, you must first seek its source and inquire therein. Depending on your particular philosophical or spiritual bent, you may simply seek the truth of wisdom at its very essence, or inquire of the author of that particular truth, living or dead. In any case, wisdom is truth. Truth is truth. It is an absolute. It is not relative. Understanding it will save you a lot of heartache and grief, but only if you have made it your own – *before* applying knowledge.

OK, now let's talk about knowledge (finally.) Knowledge is a collection of facts. Facts are true. In the proper context, they enable correct, proper and effective action. Out of order, or context, they will lead you on a merry chase… of your tail. When aligned with the understanding of wisdom, it becomes quite obvious which facts are applicable and which ones are irrelevant. Stating the obvious is therefore directly enabled by having wisdom, understanding and knowledge, in that particular order.

Period.

annoying

[Note: *For those of you who still insist on dropping immediately to the granular level; there you have it. You can now run along your merry way without reading the rest of the book. (P.S. There are no shortcuts.) For those of us who really want to learn how to reveal the obvious… keep reading.*]

See, I told you I was the most annoying person you'll ever meet. I kept my promise. That's integrity. Yet another of my annoying characteristics. But, we'll cover integrity later.

obvious annoying CHECKLIST
☐ Reveal the obvious truth.
☐ Not for the faint of heart.
☐ It's all in the way you say it.
☐ Experience happened to you. Wisdom is somebody else's experience.
☐ Wisdom/Understanding/Knowledge. In that order. Period.
☐ Integrity is a symptom of revealing the obvious.

notes: _____

chap 2

Occam had a Razor

Yup, he sure did. And he used it to shave a circular bald spot on the top of his head. Of course, that was fashionable for monks in the 13th century. What wasn't so fashionable was going against established scientific dogma to propose elegant simplicity as the best arbiter of a philosophical or scientific solution. Sounds pretty high-falutin' to me, Pardner...

Well actually, it kinda' is. Here's the technical version for the people who just can't leave well enough alone. (Mere mortals can skip the definition. You won't miss anything that isn't already obvious...)

Definition of Occam's Razor

- *"a scientific and philosophical rule that entities should not be multiplied unnecessarily which interpreted as requiring that the simplest of competing theories be preferred to the more complex or that explanations of unknown phenomena should be sought first in terms of known quantities."*

In simple terms, "The simplest and most direct solution is generally the best." Stick to the obvious.

Sir Arthur Conan Doyle[16] spoke the same concept about the obvious through Sherlock Holmes[17] when he said, "When you have eliminated the impossible, whatever remains, however improbable, must be the truth." Different side of the same coin.

And ye olde William of Ockham[18] tended to look at everything through that filter, as well. After all, it's his razor. A little simplistic, but that's the point. It's obvious.

Imagine if British automotive engineers had ascribed to that basic tenet. We never would have seen, let alone paid for the excruciating repair of the 1963 Jaguar XKE rear end. Nor would it have kept mechanics of "collectible" British sports cars in business for generations. Nor would we have endured the esoteric differences between Baroque[19] and Rococo[20] in Art History 101, after lunch, in winter, in a darkened room with a slide projector *[Ed. Note: predates video projectors and death by PowerPoint]* humming us into somnambulistic[21] delirium. And who can forget the ever-popular directions from Ikea[22]? But, I digress…

Simple is better.

the obvious path

Simplicity and directness are obviously a better solution. Always have been. It takes humankind to muddy it up with extraneous details and inscrutable processes. All to validate our own self-worth. Aha! Another obvious clue. Creating or choosing a complicated solution is merely a means of false validation of self. It places the focus on the person instead of the objective. Much akin to the "ad hominem[23]" argument, which states, "If you're losing the argument, attack the person instead of the issue." "Well, since you won't accept my argument, I contend you're ugly and your Mother dresses you funny. So, there." Just another false validation of self, and so transparent it's obvious to all but the perpetrator of the personal attack. Point out that obvious fact sometime and see what happens. By keeping the discussion focused on the issue as opposed to the persons involved in the debate, obviosity always gains the upper hand. Check and mate.

However, obvious simplicity is not to be confused with "Farm Geometry." Now we all remember 8th grade geometry when we learned the shortest distance between two points – a straight line. Right? Except on a farm. To simply move one of those big round bales of hay out to the pasture for the epicurean[24] delight of a herd

of voracious[25] bovines[26], is not a straight line. Oh no, no, no. Au contraire[27]! You must first move the mower that is blocking the tractor. To do that you must first put gas in it and then get a battery to start the recalcitrant[28] internal-combustion engine of the mower. Then you have to make room for the mower to "go somewhere else," preferably out of the path of the tractor. Then you must start the tractor (which is 6V, not 12V, See previous process for starting the mower – with a different battery.) Then you must attach the hay spike which requires BIG tools that are up in the other barn. After getting the spike attached and the tractor started you must negotiate several gates and keep the other livestock in their respective domains, all the while avoiding running over them (Mama frowns on that.) Finally, you get the bale on the spike and head over to the target pasture and negotiate that gate while keeping the now ravenously hungry and anxiously enthusiastic bossies at bay. Then, and only then, can you drop the bale in the feeder (so they don't poop all over it while eating.) Simple (kinda'...) Direct? Nope. That is "Farm Geometry."

It has many cousins; "Diaper Bag Geometry," "Camping Geometry," "Significant Other's Birthday Geometry." etc. The list

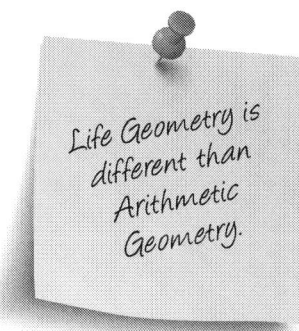

Life Geometry is different than Arithmetic Geometry.

is endless. A straight line exists only in the sterile confines of arithmetic academia and geometric theorem. The rest of us live in the real world. And it's messy. So what's the obvious solution?

Ahh. Well done, Grasshopper[29]. Once again, you're asking the right question. Finding the obvious solution is the elegantly simple task of dissociating from the noise of the world around us and simply looking at the situation through fresh and unencumbered eyes. The solution will be readily apparent. It's obvious.

We have been trained all our lives to flounder in all the superficial detritus[30] of this world as a way of solving problems. When, in fact, the solution is much simpler. It may have steps. There may be many. But the way is clear when viewed with Occam's Razor as your guide.

Simplicity has long been an ideal of humankind. One need only to look at the Stoics[31] of ancient Greece, the Ascetics[32] of the Protestant Reformation[33], the Zen Buddhists[34] of Asian antiquity, the poets Whitman[35], Whittier[36], cummings[37], the anonymous writers of Haiku[38], the mid 20th century "Minimalists[39]," or even the "100 Items Movement[40]" or tiny house[41] afficionados. Simplicity is a tauntingly elusive ideal

Simplicity is an elusive ideal. Chase it anyway...

[B]

paradigm. It's always tantalizingly "just out of reach," except to the hallowed few who have been able to escape the thrall[42] of the current. When in fact, all they are simply seeking is to be in tune with the obvious.

OK. So, let's be obvious.

Good creativity is simple. Achingly so. So much so, it becomes excruciatingly beautiful in its simplicity. Over in Switzerland back in the early 20th century, a group of artists were so struck by this obvious epiphany[43] that they even started an entire school of art in its honor. Bauhaus[44]. And as with all beautifully fundamental creative paradigms, it quickly spread to other disciplines where the other artists, artisans, craftsmen and mere mortals lived. "Less is more" became the movement's battle cry. And the basic tenets of the school blossomed and grew until they became invisible in the relentless rush of humanity to make everything the same. Flat, innocuous[45] uniformity. But, new and spontaneous devotees still occasionally rise up when they encounter the obvious beauty of simplicity in design and living. They flourish for a while until the tide of similitude simply overwhelms them and they soundlessly sink into oblivion. (Cut to black) Whew! That was kinda' dark, wasn't it?

The good news is that the obvious beauty of simplicity is totally irrepressible. It cannot be stopped or destroyed. It can only be covered for the briefest of moments until somebody comes along and sees the

The obvious will reveal itself. What are you going to do with it?

obvious sticking up from the mud. It's not new, but its rediscovery is. And the person who rediscovers it has just grasped a brief glimpse of the obvious. They can keep that brilliant nano-moment to themselves, or they can release it to the astonishment of others around them. No. They didn't see it. You did. It was obvious to you. They looked at it, but nobody "saw" it.

Now it's your responsibility.

Do you cover it back over with the mud of irrelevance and cherish it in your heart as a shining sparkle of revelation? Or do you reveal the obvious?

Once upon a time in merry olde England there lived an English engineer who saw the obvious. He went against all convention and relentlessly sought simplicity in an absurdly complicated world; Formula 1. He stringently fought against prevailing design theory and founded his style on the multi-purposing of every part he designed and built. Unless a part served three distinct purposes/functions, it was redesigned. He was the first race car designer to make the engine a stressed structural member thereby saving all the weight of that section of the frame. (Remember: Speed in racing is all about the weight-to-horsepower ratio. Less weight gives you more usable horsepower.) Then instead of using the traditional tube frames in his cars, he was a pioneer in monocoque[46] construction (panels connected by edges in a multi-faceted boxlike structure.) More weight savings. He is famously quoted as saying, "Adding horsepower makes you faster in the straights. Subtracting weight makes you faster everywhere."

Then he turned his attention to this new-fangled, aerodynamics craze. After all, the air presented an exponentially increasing drag on the car as it tore through the atmosphere. Getting the power to the road became increasingly difficult as his cars became lighter and lighter. "So, obviously I need to make the aerodynamics work to my advantage," he thought. So he did.

Formula 1 is a game of rules, made up by the French. And we all know how well the English get along with the French. For Colin Chapman[47], it was a delightful and invigorating challenge. Some little American chemical company named DuPont[48] came up with this "greasy" translucent, white plastic that slipped on everything, kinda' like PTFE[49] (Teflon[50].) They called it "Delrin[51]." So Colin put air dams with the bottom edge made of Delrin on the sides of his vehicles that were spring loaded and actually made continuous contact with the ground. At speed, this contact made an air channel under the car that actually sucked it down to the road, with negligible additional drag. The cars could now run mind-bendingly fast through the turns and gave him a significant advantage over all the other racers. The French rulemakers lost their minds.

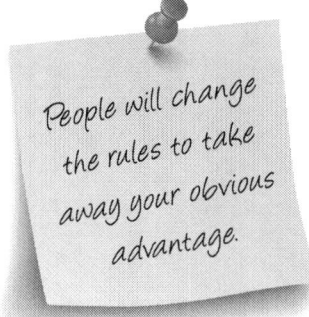

The following year they changed the rules to eliminate Colin's advantage. Now, all the racers would be checked as they left and entered the pits for enough clearance to defeat his aerodynamic advantage. Obviously, he took this as a challenge and re-tooled. Since his racers all had monocoque chassis, they were independent of the body. Sooooo… Colin just attached his side air dams to the body and put the body on hydraulic lifters. Voila[52]! Now when his sleek, black beauties left the pits, the body was 5 cm. off the ground. By the time it had gone around the track once, the dams were making contact with the ground. Upon returning to the pits, he reversed the process. Again, he was coloring inside the lines, kicking assets and the French lost their minds, again.

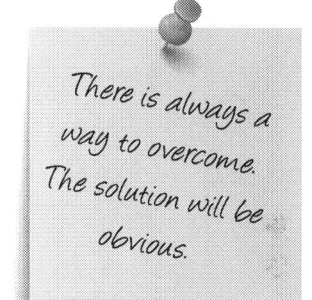

There is always a way to overcome. The solution will be obvious.

They changed the rules again the next year. No more "moveable bodies." So Colin went in the next obvious direction, Horsepower. Since all the engines had to have the same cubic displacement (size), Colin looked at improving the air intake. Cold air is denser than hot air (next to the track) so he put a vertical scoop high over the engine which allowed him to get more dense, cold air to generate higher air volume through the turbo and subsequently more horsepower than the other racers.

(P.S. I oversimplified this process and left out some extraneous techno-poop[53] you really didn't need to know.) The French lost their minds and changed the rules with a height restriction on the scoops. Colin turned his scoop horizontal and maintained dominance. The French responded as you might expect by now and changed the rules.

Colin obviously ascribed to the precept that, "Once you convince a person that they are smarter than their neighbor, there's no end to the fool you can make of them.[54]"

The following year, Colin focused on the next most obvious area to improve, fuel capacity. Everyone was restricted to the exact same size fuel tank. So, Colin super cooled his fuel with liquid nitrogen and fueled his cars right before the race started. All very legal. Super cooled fuel shrinks in size so it takes up less space in the fuel tank. More fuel in the same tank. As the fuel warmed up and expanded on the track, the engine was happily sipping away and making room for the expanded fuel. More fuel = fewer pitstops. Fewer pitstops = less time wasted. Less time wasted = more time racing. More time racing = the French losing their minds and changing the rules, again.

This process continued until Colin became bored with having a constant battle of wits with an unarmed opponent. He left Formula 1 at the top of his game and went into ultra-light planes[55]. He continued to capitalize on the obvious until his untimely death from a heart attack at 54 years of age. Live fast, die young.

"Whoa! So, what's the lesson in that?" you ask. "Be obvious, die young?"

No. By being in tune with obvious simplicity, he did everything he wanted to accomplish in the arena of his life's passion. That's called "Self-Actualization[56]" (Thank you, Mr. Maslow[57].) He had done it all and moved on to the next obvious extrapolation of his

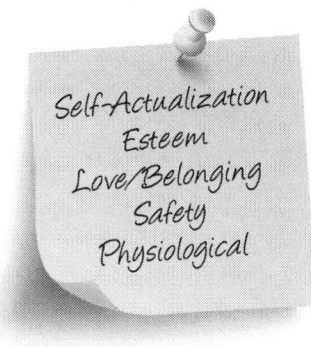

expertise; ultra-light aircraft. All the knowledge and creative principles carried over directly to his new vocation. He was living a very obvious and fulfilled life. But, when your number's up, your number's up. In the meantime, he lived life to the fullest by being obvious.

Simplicity is not solely in the purview of high-tech or engineering. Simplicity is in and of itself, beautiful. Beauty is obvious to even the merest of mortals. Only the outliers of humanity fail to respond to its presence. It doesn't have to be fancy, either. Prose can be just as beautiful as poetry and the expression of an emotion through art can be achingly beautiful in its ascetic simplicity.

One need only to look at 17th century Japanese Inns[58] to understand the beauty of simplicity. Simplicity in architecture. Simplicity in landscaping. Simplicity in art, food, hospitality and… life. The peace that overwhelms the partaker of the inn is profound in its simplicity. The craftsman's perfection of joinery in the woodwork. The recognition of natural beauty in the raw materials. The seamless integration of the outdoors and the interior. The exquisite temporal beauty of the Ikebana[59] flower arrangement to match the changing seasons and the eminently manifest "Wa[60]," the peace of the household, all contribute to being excruciatingly beautiful in the simplest of terms. Obviosity at its best.

Just as art is universal in its appeal to the higher consciousness of humankind, so one person's opinion of it is no more or less cogent or valuable than another. The opinion of the homeless person on the street in Dubuque, Iowa is no more or less valid or important than the Curator at MoMA[61] in the Big Apple[62]. Now, while the Art Majors out there peel themselves off the ceiling, let me explain.

(See, I told you there's a price to being obvious…)

If art is universal in its effect and appeal, then no one's opinion of it has more value than the other. Certainly, the Curator understands more of the nuance, history, social significance and qualitative and categorical assessment of any given piece, but the curator has just one voice – in a universal arena. Art. If the art conveys an emotion, it is good. If it conveys the emotion the artist intended, it is successful. If it conveys an emotion that transcends time and space, it is great. It will stand unflinchingly on its own merits in the gaze of generic humanity for time immemorial.

Art is Universal.

(Cue SFX: Cathedral Chorale rendition of "Ah-ah-a-a-men-n-n-n.") Creativity is always obvious in its value, or lack thereof.

The same thing is true of humor. If you have to explain the joke, it didn't work. Obviously.

obvious occam CHECKLIST

- [ ] The simplest and most direct solution is generally the best.
- [ ] A complex solution is generally false validation of self.
- [ ] Farm Geometry is how life really goes.
- [ ] Shut out the noise, and things become obvious.
- [ ] Good creativity is simple. Simple is better.
- [ ] Living obviously is fulfilling.
- [ ] If art is universal, all opinions of it are equally valid.

notes: _____

chap 3

Oblivious to the Obvious

The vast majority of the people on the planet walk around blissfully unaware of their surroundings. They neither know nor care what's going on around them. You see them everywhere. Earbuds in place, looking down, transfixed by their mobile devices and disconnected from the world at large. Or they're on Zoom looking as if they are interested in and doing anything else as long as it doesn't have to do with the reality at hand. Relying on the transcendent[63] anonymity of digital media to buffer them from what's really relevant - people. I refer to this as being in the "White Zone[64]." There are three other zones and a fourth, where you never, ever want to be.

The White Zone is not an evil place. It's just a place of total unawareness of your surroundings. It comes with a sense of peace and well-being. And by definition, that sense is totally bereft of the awareness of the reality that surrounds. If you're actually in a "safe" place, being in the White Zone is totally acceptable. In fact, it can be downright healthy and restorative – healing. But, if you're not actually in a safe place, the White Zone can be very dangerous on so many levels. Seriously dangerous. Simply because you're not aware of the obvious.

Keep in mind that EVERYBODY is in the White Zone on a

oblivious

regular basis. Ya' gotta' sleep sometime… Just preferably not when you're ambulatory[65] and at least supposedly semi-conscious. (Pre-caffeination notwithstanding.) When you are sleeping, you are blissfully unaware of your surroundings and must go through a transition when waking up. All of which leaves you out of the game. But you can't ride the pine[66] forever. You gotta' get up at some point and knock the hide off the ball[67].

The bad White Zone I'm talking about is like the example at the top of this chapter. Disconnected from your surroundings while supposedly up and functioning. Sure, I understand that we all are overwhelmed with images, messages and agendas in a relentless barrage of calculated disruption[68] in our everyday lives. We need to filter and distance ourselves from the noise. It's just that the White Zone is NOT the answer. It's downright dangerous. Life and death dangerous. Think about the person lost in their mobile device, earbuds rockin' and traversing the crosswalk while actively trying to disprove the Law of Impenetrability, (which states: "No two objects

the obvious path

oblivious

can occupy the same space at the same time.") by stepping in front of the distracted driver (texting) of a city bus. Ouch.

Don't attempt to break the laws of physics.

Really bad mojo.

A lot of bad stuff just happened here because of being in the White Zone at the wrong time, in the wrong place. And it doesn't have to be by meeting a bus by accident on a public thoroughfare. It can happen when an opportunity presents itself to you in a meeting or when you are in an online community. You're just not there and now you pay the opportunity cost[69] for the opportunity lost. How big a deal was that? I dunno'. You tell me. I think the cost is obvious.

Conversely, I'm not talking about being so hyper-alert all the time that you toast your adrenal gland while living in a constant state of "Fight or Flight[70]." No one can sustain that condition for long before crumbling into a heap of smoldering ashes. Obviously, there's got to be some middle ground here. Let's call it the "Yellow Zone."

oblivious

Keep in mind, we're talking about risk here. What you need to understand is that risk comes in two flavors: Negative and Positive[71]. Negative risks (meeting the potential future parents-in-law, driving on the freeway in L.A., putting your hand in a meat grinder) have potentially negative consequences. Positive risks (meeting the potential future parents-in-law, buying a lottery ticket, saying "I love you") have the potential of bringing great joy and benefit both tangible and intangible. (Oh, you noticed that I listed the same event in both the Positive and Negative Risk examples. Good. I was just checking to see if you were staying out of the White Zone...)

Obviously, risks can go either way. You have to be present and paying attention to the obvious in order to know which way the tree is gonna' fall. It even gives you the opportunity on occasion to help determine which way it's gonna' fall. Nice option. But it's only going to happen if you have your head in the game. In the Yellow Zone.

So, what is the Yellow Zone? It is a state of heightened awareness of one's surroundings and the overall safety level therein. Pretty simple. Ever have the hair stand up on the back of your neck in a public situation? Chances are you looked around and identified some kind of bad actor[72] or less than optimal situation. If you hadn't been in the Yellow Zone, you wouldn't have noticed and may have had to pay the price. Not being aware of the wasps' nest when you are *oblivious*

trimming the bushes can result in some wild arm waving, amazing free-style aerobics and painful consequences. The same is true of bad actors: the people who intend you harm. But, don't forget the good actors that bring with them benefit and opportunity. They're both risks. You just need to be aware in order to deal with them appropriately. These risks will be quite obvious to you when you are in the Yellow Zone.

OK. So now you're in the Yellow Zone and most of your surroundings are pretty obvious to you. Good for you. You should live in Yellow. It looks good on you. But, now you've identified a threat or opportunity. You should be assessing how to respond at this point. It generally happens in microseconds. Enhance[73] the opportunity or mitigate[74] the threat. You have now just passed the threshold into the Orange Zone. You have identified the risk. You have determined if it's an opportunity or a threat. And you are formulating an immediate plan of action. You're like a sprinter in the blocks waiting for the starter's gun to go off. The next step is quite obvious.

Don't try to "figure it out" in the Red Zone. Plan Ahead!

The Red Zone. Game on. This is where you respond with all the APPROPRIATE energy and action for the given situation. Screaming, "AND I LOVE YOU, TOO!!!" may be way more energy than the situation calls for. A simple look and gentle touch may be all that's necessary. Conversely, yanking the toddler's hand away (and consequently the rest of the toddler) from the blazing, red hot, BBQ grill may be totally appropriate. But immediate action is the obvious key. No need to belabor the point. It's obvious.

Now, like I said, there's one more Zone I need to mention. The Brown Zone. It's when your head is in a warm, dark, moist place that isn't physiologically possible. Never be in the Brown Zone. It's MUCH more dangerous than the White Zone. Trust me. I know. From first-hand experience.

Sadly, most people spend the majority of their time in the White Zone. That's because they're basically unaware and will mock anyone who points out that fact to them. (I can hear some of you groaning right now...) But revealing the obvious always comes with a cost and more often than not, a benefit, too. That's the risk. People will mock the articulation of the obvious because, "I already knew that." Or they will take offense at having a light shone into an area of their life that they would prefer to remain dark. People tend to prefer the darkness. The light is obvious and makes other things obvious, too. Be prepared for the responses, They could go either way.

So, how do you decide which obvious things to note and which to let lay unaddressed? Wisdom. As you become increasingly aware of the obvious, you will need a guide to help you determine the right way, place and time to articulate what is so abundantly clear to you. Oh, there are other obstacles to revealing the obvious, too. Insecurity is one of them.

oblivious

People tend to think that what's obvious to them must certainly be obvious to others. Wrong. But, their insecurities about the value and uniqueness of what they see as being so very obvious will stop them from ever saying a word. Honest Abe[75] is quoted as saying, "It is better to be thought a fool and remain silent than to open one's mouth and remove all doubt." But, I contend that wisdom is often thought to be foolishness by those who lack understanding. Wisdom can defend itself. Wisdom is obvious. Just reveal the obvious in clear and unambiguous terms. The tree may fall in the direction of your preference, but the chips will fall wherever they may. Exposed foolishness is just the collateral damage of revealing the obvious.

Keep your words sweet. You may have to eat them.

Then there's the obstacle of having to eat humble pie. Revealing the obvious often encompasses one's necessity to change a personal paradigm. You will have to have the courage to be willing to endure the mockery of others when you reveal an obvious truth that stands in direct opposition to a position you previously held. You will have to have the courage to change… and grow. Revealing the obvious is not easy or comfortable. But the good news is, "Your comfort zone will kill you." Fortunately for you, you can avoid that and have decided by this point to "give this 'obvious thing' a go." Just remember: "There is no try. Only do."

What is obvious to you is NOT obvious to others. Yes, it takes courage to be aware of, let alone reveal the obvious. But, the

oblivious

rewards far outweigh the risks. People who once were put off by you for shaking or shattering their paradigms through revealing the obvious, will begin seeking you out and your advice (read: wisdom.) Surprising people. People who you never thought would respond to you, let alone positively. That's the beauty of "obviosity." It is unassailable on so many levels. It can defend itself because frankly, it's obvious. Only a fool would deny it. And the world is full of fools. Don't be one.

> Becoming a "5 Percenter" is just a decision.

As you've probably figured out by now in your life, it doesn't take much to stand out from the crowd. Being a doer immediately puts you in that 5% that rise to the top. Just consistently making the effort toward an identified goal pays tremendous rewards to the diligent. Talent only goes so far. Good looks fade. Gravity is not our friend. Intelligence is highly overrated. So, what makes the difference? Deciding to do, and being consistently persistent. We all know the cool kids from high school who ended up burnt out and washed up by the first class reunion and the "ordinary" kids who picked a trade and now live in the big house and are doing so well on so many levels that it defies the imagination. There was a kid in my elementary school class who was from a traditional Macedonian family and we became childhood friends. After high school he got ahold of "this computer thing," as he described it at our first high school reunion, and subsequently became a multi-multi-millionaire. Jimmy Bidzos[76] owns ".com[77]". He did OK for himself by owning the obvious.

oblivious

Plain or sparkly doesn't make the difference. Obviously, persistence does. I wish I had some pithy aphorism to offer you about it to you now, but that's just it. Persistence pays. Now apply that to revealing the obvious.

Finally, now that you decided to distinguish yourself from the other 95% of humanity and have committed to revealing the obvious, how do you get the rubber to the road... consistently? First you have to realize that the creative genius that dwells within you is inexhaustible. Embrace it. Live it. Share it with others. The ones who respond positively are also aware of the creative genius that lives within them. It's obvious to both of you.

By courageously embracing the obvious, you free yourself up to act on the wisdom you now understand. The clarity you will experience is deafening. It will drown out all the clutter and noise of the clamorous world around you. You will be able to see clearly in complex and overgrown situations. You've always been able to see the obvious. It was always there. Are you willing to admit that you were wrong before and embrace the obvious truth in front of you? That's where the courage comes in. That's where you embark on an adventure that will take you places few people are willing to go or even dreamed existed. It's an obvious adventure.

Are you ready?

oblivious

obvious oblivious CHECKLIST

- [ ] Most people are completely unaware.
- [ ] Know the zones: White/Yellow/Orange/Red.
- [ ] Stay out of the Brown Zone.
- [ ] People will mock you for being obvious.
- [ ] Insecurity blocks obviosity.
- [ ] Risk eating humble pie.
- [ ] Be persistently and consistently obvious.
- [ ] It will take courage to be obvious. Embrace it.

notes:

chap 4

"But, I'm not creative."

"I can't even draw a straight line."

So, what.

"But, you don't understand. People can't even recognize my stick people."

Don't care.

You're still creative no matter what so-called "evidence" to the contrary that you can present to me. I contend that you are creative. But, more than that, I am absolutely certain that you have creativity residing within you.

Let me explain. I remember the first time I bumped into the concept of my own creativity. Based on my recollection of which house we were living in at the time, I must have been between 3 and 4 years old. I had just finished my latest masterpiece; a portrait of a cardinal (the bird, not the guy with the little red hat[78].) It was a magnificent piece by my estimation and a visitor in our home concurred.

creative

"That's a beautiful picture of a cardinal," he said. Perhaps the brilliant red color and the red triangle on the top of its head was a dead giveaway. I had certainly given the ol' Red Crayola[79] a workout on this one. Worked it right to the bone. I didn't want anyone to mistake what color my cardinal was.

"You could be a commercial artist someday." He had piqued my interest, as much as one can pique anything on a 4 year old.

"What's that?"
I innocently responded.

"Oh, they draw pictures all day and people pay them for it."

Epiphanies happen at any age.

I knew in that moment that my life's trajectory had been set. "That's for me." I said in my little head and cherished the notion from that point forward.

But I also had a transformational epiphany at that point. One

the obvious path

creative

that far overshadowed my lifetime career choice. I also realized in that moment that this really cool creative talent thing was coming from somewhere else. It just happened and flowed through my fingers and onto the paper (and the surrounding table and sometimes the wall if I was feeling particularly free and unencumbered.) But the point was: it was coming from a transcendent[80] source. Some place "other than" me. I had control of it, but not really. If I tried to grasp it too firmly, it would melt into vapor and float away through my fingers. I could only hold it in the gentlest of terms and let it, not me, pour forth the beauty. It became my best and most extraordinary friend.

It wasn't until much later that I figured out, because of this creative thing that I had, that other people don't think like I do. Or see the world the same way as I do. But, the creative thing was different and identical, all at the same time.

"How does that work?" I wondered. Then I looked more closely at the similarities between my "creative thing," and other people's. They had creative expressions that I marvelled

creative

at and yet, they marvelled at mine. Music, for instance. I could be a very technically proficient player of an instrument, but I'm not sure I could ever be a musician. They amaze me. They just think and the music flows with such beauty and emotion that I become transfixed in the moment. They simply are and the music flows out from them. They don't even think about it. It's nothing short of miraculous. After numerous attempts at playing an instrument (recorder, accordion, violin, piano, 5-string banjo) I decided I would never be a musician. They have something very special that I don't have. So, I stuck to the only instrument I was good at; I play the radio.

One time, I had the privilege of working with a Microsoft MVP (of which there were only 5 in the US at that time.) When he typed, it sounded like frying bacon. Blindingly fast. And he was writing code! Astounding! I would stand transfixed and stare over his shoulder as line after line appeared in a string faster than I could read it. When I marvelled at his skill, he just shrugged and said, "Well, you need to type if you write code." This was not writing code. This was becoming one with the machine.

the obvious path

What's easy for you amazes others.

I would slink back to my desk and get back to doing design work on my computer, only to sense a presence over my shoulder. Turning around, I was surprised to see him standing transfixed and staring at my screen. "How do you do that? It's incredible!" he blurted out. I shrugged and said, "It's what I do." We immediately formed our own mutual appreciation consortium, complete with big funny hats and a secret handshake. Fred and Barney[81] had nothing on us. (Neither did Ralph and Ed[82], for that matter.)

But, creativity is not in any way limited to the arts. (Once again, somebody give a paper bag to the Art Majors and have them breathe into it. They're starting to hyperventilate.) My question became, "What's art got to do with it?" Speaking of Art, he always used to say, "You have to be creative to be an artist, but you don't have to be an artist to be creative." It seems people tend to confuse artistic ability with creative ability. That's elitist and I am not.

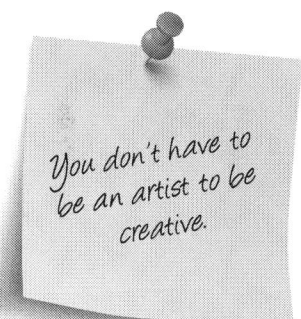

You don't have to be an artist to be creative.

I was seeing creativity everywhere I looked. Who came up with the Zip-Loc[83] bag let alone Velcro[84]? Why isn't the person who invented duct tape ruling the world? How did they get

creative

Teflon to stick to pans, when nothing sticks to Teflon? My childish curiosity has never failed me. Now I am astounded by how the articulated joint on the Keurig[85] works and how my computer senses my frustration level and arbitrarily shuts down a feature or sub-routine in response. Somebody thought of those things and brought them into reality. Creative people. People who can do stuff I can't even imagine, effortlessly. Just because it's who they are and what they do.

Creativity comes in every flavor and a few that aren't. That's just it, somebody is going to have to think of that flavor and make it happen. Maybe it's you. I don't know. Do you?

Each of us recognizes that there are things that are easy and clear to us, that other people just don't see. The guy who invented the safety pin[86] was just idly bending a piece of wire while sitting in the Patent Office waiting room to get another of his inventions patented. What about the Flow-Bee[87]? Or the first guy that thought a raw oyster must be food? And what about "Happy Accidents"? Post-It notes came out of a "failed" adhesive[88]. Charlie Goodyear[89] accidentally dropped sulphur in a pot of molten goo and created an entire industry based on "Vulcanized Rubber[90]." Were these just accidents or did they just realize the obvious value of what was directly in front of them? I vote for the latter.

Happy Accidents are the things that make fortunes for people.

Stay Alert!

They all saw something that other people saw, but didn't "see." It was quite obvious to them. And by speaking up, and bringing that ridiculous idea to fruition, we now have marvelous things all around us in our daily lives. Now, which of those things was truly artistic? Probably very, very few if any at all. Perhaps with the exception of the Flow-Bee. I love the Flow-Bee. I just have no use for it now. (See Bio Pic at the end of the book.)

If you still don't think you're creative, just think about some of the stories you came up with regarding why you didn't have your homework or why you were going 57 in a 35 zone. All creative thoughts. Some created under pressure, some with planning. Much like the time I went to chemistry class on fire.

Everyone has those teachers in school. The ones that everybody knows are "tough'" and demanding. Nobody wanted to be in their class. They always wanted the "other" teacher. In my high school, it was Mrs. Hoffman. She taught chemistry. And you would learn... or else. Well, at the beginning of every school year she would give the same speech to her fresh crop of ritual sacrifices.

"You WILL always turn in your homework, complete and on time, AND... You will NEVER ever be late for my class. If you ever have the misfortune to be late, you must do two

creative

things: 1. You will have a signed and time-stamped note from the office stating why you are late, and 2. You will stand up in front of the entire class and tell a story about why you were late – without a word of truth in it." She was convinced she had covered all the bases. What she hadn't anticipated was… me.

I almost melted. This challenge must have been written especially for me. I had found my raison d'etre[91]. It may have daunted the generations that came before me in their endless, fatalistically forced trudge through these hallowed and angst ridden halls, but the gauntlet had been thrown[92]. "I accept!"

I had fulfilled all my fiduciary responsibilities[93] as a Hoffmanian Acolyte through all four semesters with a 4.0 in the class. The last day was rapidly approaching, and I was prepared. All we had to do was turn in our books and clean up the lab on this final, fateful day. The final exam had been taken. The grades were sealed. Nothing could change that now. It was my chance. My moment of glory.

For months in advance, I had "appropriated" several necessary items; a 6 in. square of asbestos for putting under flaming Bunsen burners[94] from the chem lab (Yes, asbestos, they didn't know any better back in the Pleistocene age[95]. We handled Mercury, too. None of us died. Go figure.) a

creative

wood screw, an arrow from the varsity archery range, the top of a tin can, some twine, an old flannel shirt, some gauze bandage, a can of Energine[96] (primarily toluene, extraordinarily flammable) some thread, and of course... stage blood from the drama department. Lots of it.

I put the screw through the tin can lid, then the asbestos pad, then the flannel shirt and finally into the end of the feather half of the arrow. I tied the contraption very securely around my chest with the twine, with the arrow sticking straight out of the center of my back. And as the man who fell off the ten-story building was heard to say as he passed the third floor window, "So far, so good."

I buttoned up the shirt and tucked it in my pants. Then I had my accomplice (trusting soul) liberally douse the area around the base of the arrow with stage blood. No need to catch on fire, eh? (My Momma drowned all the stupid ones. I did OK once I got out of the bag...) The final addition was the gauze pad tied at the base of the arrow where it entered my back. Then the pièce de résistance[97], the Energine. I asked John to douse the gauze with it and couldn't accurately ascertain his enthusiasm for the job because my back was already wet from the stage blood. In retrospect, perhaps this part shouldn't have been done

Things never really go as planned... Be flexible.

creative

without adult supervision.

The clock ticked. I was now 20 minutes late for class. There would be no mistaking that I was, in fact, truly late. All systems "Go." I leaned forward so my beautiful locks (Yes, I had hair. Thank you for asking.) wouldn't go up in flames. "Light me." There was the momentary pause, the Zippo[98] leaped to life and the Energine ignited with a surprisingly basso profundo[99], "Whoomph!". I noticed out of the corner of my eye that the entire hall lit up. "My, that's a lot of light from that little bit of gauze on my back," I mused. But I couldn't think about that now. "It's Show time!"

As time slowed down to a barely perceptible trickle forward, I threw open the door, grabbed the door jamb and clutched my chest with the other hand and screamed –

"Mrs. Hoffman!! Comanches!!!"

And fell to the floor with flames rising majestically up to the ceiling. The surrounding students shrieked as they back-climbed up onto their desks and recoiled from the impromptu conflagration that had interrupted their mundane little day in chem lab. As I lay there in that moment of sweet perfection, my back began to get warm. Very warm. A thought flooded my consciousness, "This is perhaps… No, this IS the dumbest thing I have ever done." Then I turned my attention to another pressing thought.

creative

"Where's John with that damp towel to put me out?"

By this time, Mrs. Hoffman was running frantically back and forth at the front of the classroom, until she gathered her wits about her and grabbed the fire extinguisher and disassociated it from the wall. Not released, mind you, but bracket and all. Then in true Marion Robert Morrison[100]-style, she yanked the pin from the fire extinguisher and aimed the black cone of cloudy fury straight at my back.

Believe in your plan. Wholeheartedly.

But just as fate would have it, John arrived mere nano-seconds before she pulled the trigger, and he calmly put out the fire with the damp towel. Fait accompli[101]. But wait! There's more! Operators are standing by. Have your Visa or MasterCard ready. This offer will not be repeated. I repeat: This offer will not be repeated!

Mrs. Hoffman turned on her heel and returned the fire extinguisher (and still firmly attached bracket) to her desk and set it down with an unceremonious thud. While trying heroically to control her breathing and in anticipation of all the students returning to their desks in the proscribed manner, she regained her composure. The air was silent and deathly still.

creative

"Very well, Mr. Buck. May I have your note, please?"

Ahh, but I was prepared. I deftly reached into the unburned pocket on the front of my now smoldering flannel shirt and produced the note. Official. Time-Stamped. And signed by the school nurse, Mr. Franks (who was a dear friend of Mrs. Hoffman and in on the incendiary extravaganza.)

She politely received my note and read it aloud to the class after clearing her throat.

"Please forgive Steve's tardiness. It seems he's had an attack."

She calmly folded the note, thanked me and put it in the pocket of her lab apron. Then she asked me politely to take my seat. The rest of the class went off without a hitch. To the day she retired, on the first day of every new class, she would give the same speech about her two rules and then recount the tale of the day Steve Buck came to class on fire. She would then severely admonish everyone to NOT attempt to punk the system, unless they "could come up with something better than that." No one ever did. (Imagine what would happen if some kid tried that now. The whole school would be locked down, SWAT would swarm the building and a full-blown HazMat team would be dispatched to the scene for what would

creative

ultimately be deemed a Super Fund Cleanup Site[102] by the EPA[103].) Ahh, life was simple then.

Everybody is creative.

Think about the solutions you've come up with in every facet of your life. Big ones. Small ones. Simple. Complicated. What about the times you've seen somebody struggling with something and the creative solution is quite obvious to you. Creativity is obvious... to you. Some of us have high internal clock speeds and others, slow. Your clock speed has no relation to your intelligence, creativity or ability to see the obvious. The fast ones seem to be sparkly and the slow ones, mundane. But do you really want a sparkly one to do your taxes, or the mundane one to do your hair? No. Everyone and everything in its time and for its purpose. We can't survive without any of them. Your gifts, talents and abilities are absolutely mission-critical for the world around you. Everyone is creative. Everyone is unique and everyone is needed. You just need to get in touch with the creative genius inside you and share its obviosity with the world at large. Every day.

We are all creative by nature. For example, you look a lot like your parents. And setting aside the metaphysical, they created you. Granted, your Mother contributed the blood sweat and tears and Dad just contributed to the fun part. But, they both contributed to your creation. And since the apple doesn't fall far from the tree, you can create stuff (and other people,) too. Not much of a stretch.

Life is inexhaustible and goes on with or without us. That being the case, so does creativity. Whatever you believe the source of life to be on this planet, we can all agree that it is irrepressible and relentlessly ongoing. It cannot be utterly destroyed. But even from the darkest ebb, it will reemerge triumphant. Undaunted. Eternal. You are part of that. It is part of you. Tap into it.

And with this undeniable creativity in each of us, comes tools, skills, talents and abilities that are totally unique to each of us. A little of Mom. A little of Dad. And they each had a little of their Mom and a little of their Dad. Ad infinitum[104]. Ad nauseum[105]. We just can't escape our own special, unique brand of creativity. And this unique brand of creativity is what makes different stuff obvious to each of us.

How obvious is that?

creative

obvious creative CHECKLIST

- [ ] Art is not the only arbiter of creativity.
- [ ] Thinking of stuff doesn't make you a genius. The creative genius inside you makes you think of stuff.
- [ ] Everyone is creative.
- [ ] Never go to chemistry class on fire.
- [ ] You are creative by definition.
- [ ] Your creativity is inexhaustible and it never gets tired.
- [ ] Your unique brand of creativity makes things uniquely obvious to you.

notes:

chap 5

Trust is the Key

Trust is risky business. It is the foundation of all intimacy. Without it you cannot have intimacy on any level. So, to understand intimacy, you must first understand its levels They are progressive.

LEVEL 1: Informational. "What time is it?" "It's 3:15." "Thanks!" "You're welcome." Very shallow. Very superficial. Very Non-threatening. No risks. Just information exchange.

LEVEL 2: THEIR Beliefs and Opinions. Just a trial balloon. Still no risk of exposing one's self. "I had a boss one time who always said..." Or, "They seem to want us to believe..." You gently posit a point and see what their reaction is - Without revealing your own position. Still safe.

LEVEL 3: Your own Personal Beliefs and Opinions. This is where the rubber just barely starts touching the road. You're sticking your little toe in the water to see if you're going to actually get in. "I just have a really hard time with..." Or, "I really like the way ..." This can be guised in terms of third parties or esoteric concepts and values... or as your own personal beliefs. But, it's still your opinions or beliefs. Very risky in this age of political correctness.

Or you could state how you feel about the other person's behavior (as separate and distinct from them as a person.) "I'm really impressed by how you can…" "It makes me feel smart when you break it down like that." We're starting to see that courage plays a part in intimacy.

LEVEL 4: Your own Personal Experiences and Paradigms.
Now we're starting to open the kimono[106]. Personal experiences are undeniably yours. Then, your beliefs that come as a result of those experiences, begin to paint a clearer picture of how you became who you are. An insight into your very soul (mind, will and emotions.) It's starting to get very real.

LEVEL 5: Your own Needs, Desires, Dreams and Emotions.
This reveal is indelible. Once you show it, it can't be unseen. This is where you share what is very real, deep and personal to you.

Now that you are beginning to grasp the 5 Levels of Intimacy, the components of Trust start to become very obvious. Trust is a simple concept, but don't think for a moment that it's easy.

the obvious path

trust

Especially if you've been burned before. Like the rest of us…

Consider how the following steps of Trust loosely follow the Levels of intimacy. They don't fall in a nice, neat little package (but, very little in life actually does…) Just read along and follow the progression.

Get intimate with your creativity.

1. Trust is the foundation of all intimacy. On every level.

In order to get close to someone, you're going to have to trust them. You need to trust that they won't fly away at the drop of a hat, nor will they fail you when the chips are down or stab you in the back and twist the knife, even though experience has taught you otherwise. First and foremost, you must decide to trust them… to some degree.

2. There is a difference between trusting a person and trusting their behavior.

Just as it is a fatal mistake to confuse a person with their behavior, you must understand that trusting a person and trusting their

behavior are also two different things. You can trust someone's behavior without trusting the person (a negative example.) AND... you can trust a person, but not trust their behavior. You can trust your 5 year old as a person, but not to carry the Baccarat Crystal[107] to the table for Thanksgiving. Trusting the person is what we're talking about here. People are real. Their essence is eternal. Behavior is transient. Never confuse the two.

3. Like them and believe that they like you.

People can sense when you like them and conversely feel it when you dislike them. The cues are microscopic and as subtle as pheromones[108]. But they're real, nonetheless. Don't fake it. Just "Like" them (and I don't mean click some button on social media.) Then all the subconscious cues say that your barriers are down and you're actually (gasp) vulnerable. And if you already believe that they like you, you will miss their non-verbal defenses and step inside the perimeter. You're almost there.

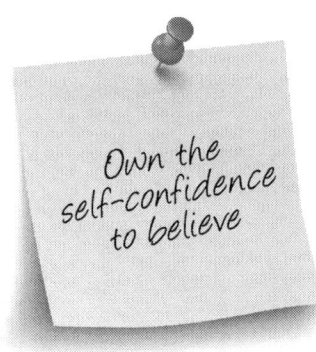
Own the self-confidence to believe

4. Believe you will be received and not harmed.

Simple acceptance is a huge motivator. If you believe you will be received, you're not giving off any signals that there is reason for reservation. We've all been around an abused dog who flinches at your every move. If you don't really believe you will be harmed, you won't flinch. You are demonstrating trust... first.

5. Reciprocation builds a bond. Once broken, is difficult to rebuild.

It's all about give and take. You have to do both. If you don't give, you're perceived as too guarded or even stingy. If you don't take, you're saying you don't want to be "indebted." Neither behavior sends the message of trust. Trust is built much like a 3-D printer. Layer upon layer. Again and again until the form emerges and the piece becomes complete. Except that it is as dimensionally stable as glass and just as brittle. It must be protected to retain its beauty. It can be rebuilt if broken, but the result is never the same as the original, pristine piece. Certainly something worth preserving.

6. Be willing to disregard what you superficially perceive, and believe they will be true to their character.

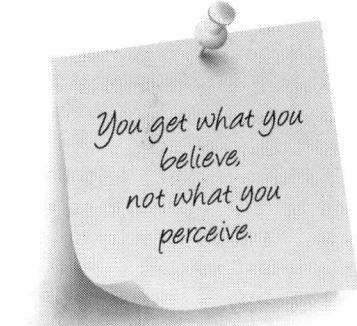

Seeing is not believing. What you see is NOT what you get. Never make literary assessments based on the aesthetic qualities of dust jackets[109]. What's external is most likely behavior. You're interested in the person. Find out about the person despite the fact that they wear Hawaiian shirts and Crocs with socks. They may be a really wonderful person even if half of their head is shaved and the rest is chartreuse. As you learn about a person, you will learn about their character ("What they do when no one is looking.") It will most certainly surprise and often delight you. Pull your head out of the box and get to know them.

They probably think you're kinda' odd, too. But you're probably both pretty true to your character.

7. Believe they are worthy of your trust.

If you've ever had an investment portfolio, you've heard or read the words, "Past performance does not guarantee future results." Which, if you think about it for a moment, is the definition of insanity. At least according to Ol' Uncle Al[110], when he said, "The definition of insanity is to continue the same behavior and expect different results." Perhaps he believed the stock market was sheer insanity, or why else would he go on to say, "Compound Interest is the Eighth Wonder of the World." Well, the Rule of 72[111] never stopped anyone from getting a high interest credit card, now did it? (He said sheepishly while feeling the MasterCard[112] mock him from his hip pocket.) You have to believe that irrespective of their past behavior, they are worthy of your trust. It is the triumph of hope over experience. Gibbs[113] had four wives. Trust the person once you know their character. Then you'll know how to trust their behavior, good or bad.

8. Be willing to risk vulnerability.

Vulnerability is letting down your guard, opening the Kimono, leading with your chin[114], saying "I love you." Vulnerability is a major component of trust. It is absolutely mission-critical for trust and subsequently for intimacy – on every level. If you don't risk being vulnerable, you will never trust. If you don't trust, you will never be close.

9. Believe their promises will be kept. That they speak the truth.

Give them the benefit of the doubt. That sounds dangerously like having belief in them, but only because it is. Belief is not a blind leap. That's a fool's game. Belief is knowing the potential consequences and yet consciously choosing to act like what you believe is true. People tend to live up to what you expect and believe of them.

10. Believe that their actions will be in your best interests or at least benefit you. Or at the very least, not harm you.

Trust character, not behavior.

You can't treat them like a threat. You must believe in the good in them. They may not be "good" (whatever that means…) people, but there is undoubtedly some good in them. Find it. Believe in it. Believe that they are willing if not eager to share it with you. Remember: People tend to live up to the expectations you have of them. If you expect nothing from them, that's exactly what you'll get. Everyone wants to feel valued.

11. Be willing to depend on them.

Hear that? Can you smell it? The rubber just hit the road. You have to put your money where your mouth is. Be willing to depend on them. If by now you have developed trust, vulnerability, and some level of intimacy, you must be willing to depend on them. It's quite acceptable to communicate that you are doing so. Only the truly sociopathic[115] among us can miss the relevance of that clue. Transparency shows.

Now, let's re-read those basic tenets and substitute "creativity" for "they/them/others." I think you'll get the point.

1. Trust is the foundation of all intimacy. On every level.

If you want to discover the creative genius in your everyday life, you will have to find a way to trust it. It is worthy of your trust. But to seek any level of intimacy with your creativity, you must first trust it. One way or another.

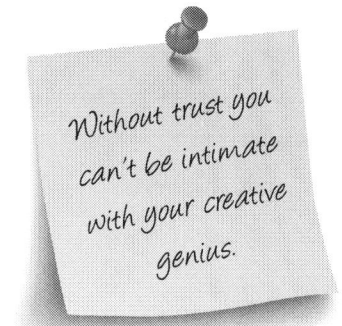

Without trust you can't be intimate with your creative genius.

2. There is a difference between trusting your creativity and trusting its behavior.

Your creative genius, that which lives inside everybody who chooses to receive it, is an entity that embodies the infinite possibilities of bringing thought into reality. It manifests itself in innumerable ways and endless permutations. Yes, you must trust your creative genius, but you can also trust its behavior. They are in total synch. That's what you call integrity. There is no guile in your creativity, only truth.

3. Like your creativity and believe that it likes you.

Approach your creativity with the full confidence that it is your friend. It likes you and is thrilled that you seek to help it manifest itself in your everyday life.

4. Believe you will be received and not harmed.

Creativity can be a little scary if you're not used to working with it directly, every day. It can even seem a little intense at first. But, that's OK. It's been bottled up in you for a long time. It's just excited to finally get a chance to manifest itself in your life. It has no intention of harming you. In fact, quite to the contrary. It has lived with your potential every day of your life and can't wait to see it come to fruition. Where you go, it goes. As you prosper and benefit, so does your creative genius.

5. Reciprocation builds a bond. Once broken, is difficult to rebuild.

The more you use it and trust it, the stronger it gets in your life. Any doubts are purely on your side. Your creative genius always believes in you, even and especially when you don't believe in it.

Believe Creativity is true.

6. Be willing to disregard what you perceive, and believe that creativity will be true to itself.

False perceptions abound about creativity. "It's just for certain people." "You have to be an artist." "You have to have gifts and talents to use it." Hogwash! Everybody has gifts and talents. And thankfully they're not the same. (Boy, wouldn't that be boring…) No! Cast aside whatever perceptions you had about creativity and perceive what is directly in front of you. It's obvious… to YOU. Creativity can't be anything but its true self.

7. Believe creativity is worthy of your trust.

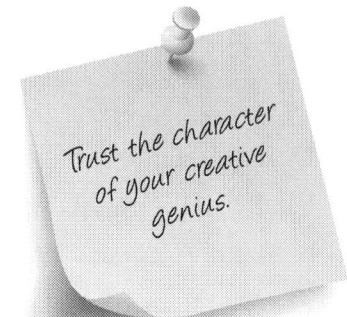

Trust the character of your creative genius.

Creativity has character and integrity. It is what it does when no one is looking and that's the same as when they are. You can trust it.

8. Be willing to risk vulnerability to your creativity.

Since you can trust your creativity, it's pretty easy (comparatively) to be vulnerable to it. Bringing forth what you know to be sincerely and truly creative is not without risk. The world is full of Neanderthals[116]. But their opinion doesn't in any way diminish the value of what you bring into reality. Your creativity transcends the opinions of others and not only expresses, but defends itself. Their criticisms are based on their own insecurities when confronted with the true value of what you bring into this corporeal realm[117]. Risk being

Be vulnerable to your creativity

vulnerable to your creative genius. It is being vulnerable to you.

9. Believe creativity's promises will be kept. That creativity speaks the truth.

Your creative genius doesn't write any checks it can't cover. Oh, you may ask or demand the wrong things from it, but it always delivers what it says it will. And it always speaks the truth.

10. Believe that creativity's actions will be in your best interests or at least benefit you. Or at the very least, not harm you.

Your creativity won't always go the way you expect it to go. In fact, it rarely does. This is where your trust comes into play. Even and especially when you can't see where it's going. That's the adventure. Your creativity will never harm you, because to harm you is to harm itself. It's not too much to say your creativity loves you.

11. Be willing to depend on your creativity.

It will always be there for you, except in one circumstance. So, you can always depend on it. Your creativity is as normal and natural for you as breathing out and breathing in. Depend on it. You don't think about your breathing, now do you? (except for right now that I mentioned it.)

If I thought for a moment that I would have to show up every day at work, as a Creative Director, and be creative, on demand, all day, every day… I would be too terrified to get out of bed, let alone go to work. It's incomprehensible. Where does it come from? Will it be there tomorrow? The next minute? Now? Terrifying.

But the good news is that your creative genius is inherent in your very being. It bubbles up through your subconscious and is inexhaustible. You are not responsible for its inception, only its application. Your subconscious never sleeps. It never gets tired. It is at the essence of your very being. And you never stop and never will. It's where dreams come from. It is the avenue, the conduit of all of your creativity.

When I first began seriously mining my creativity, I bumped into the concept that your creativity comes from your subconscious. I knew that the subconscious never sleeps and can't get tired. So, I figured that I would take advantage of those basic characteristics and burn the candle in the middle, as well as at both ends.

The source of your creativity is inexhaustible.

I had surprising results. I'm sure you thought I crashed and burned in a dazzling spectacle of sound and fury, and signifying nothing. Well, Ol' Mac[118] missed the boat on this one. I actually thrived... for a while, until the other two flames met me in the middle. But my take away was astounding; I *COULD* design in my sleep. (Now wipe that skeptical and derisive look off your face. It's not flattering to you.)

You know how when you're worried about the bills right before you fall asleep, it's also the first thing you think about when you get up? Or, if you wistfully ponder your love interest just before falling into the waiting arms of Morpheus[119], who do you think of the first thing when you wake up? Of course! Honey Bunny! Well, it works for design work, too.

My experiment began. I would list all the jobs and their design requirements I had to produce the next day and "assign" my subconscious to ruminate[120] on them throughout the night. When I would wake up in the morning, the solutions weren't TOMA[121] (Top of Mind Awareness.) But, as soon as I got to work and hit ye olde drawing boarde, the ideas just flowed. It was awesome to watch. Especially for me, since it was all coming out of my fingers right in from of me. And it didn't draw down my creativity account. If anything, it enhanced it. What finished me off was the other two ends of the candle meeting in the middle and burning me out physically. You can only do two or three "all-nighters" a week for so long before you have to pay the piper[122]. But, when you're young and stupid everything seems possible – and it is, for a while. Well, at least I'm not young anymore. I've found many new and creative ways to do stupid stuff. Just ask my wife. Like when "some woman on a plane[123]" told me I should write a book.

As we've examined before, creativity is not just one's ability in the arts, but every conscious (or unconscious) manifestation of

Assign projects to your sub-conscious.

something that didn't exist before we ushered it into existence. A thought becomes an idea and is given voice. The voice may be from our lips, our fingers or simply from the very essence that is us. We are creative. All day. Every day. It's who we are. It's what we do. (Note: Being and doing are two different things. We are human beings, not human doings.)

So, to boil it all down to something you can easily tuck in your pocket and take with you wherever you go, make these two points your very own:

A. Trust your creativity.

B. Your creativity will never betray you or harm you. It will only choose to be silent in response to your lack of trust.

(You were looking for that last part from nine paragraphs ago, weren't ya'?)

obvious trust CHECKLIST

- [ ] Trust is risky.
- [ ] Without trust there is no intimacy - on any level.
- [ ] Trust has levels.
- [ ] Trusting your creativity has the same levels.
- [ ] Your creativity won't abandon you under pressure.
- [ ] Trust your creativity, It won't betray you.

notes:

chap 6

Excellence is Imbalanced

Everyone is impressed by excellence. We all say we want to pursue it. We lift it up and put it on a pedestal. But, are we really cognizant of what we are doing? Really?

What is excellence, anyway? Something really good, right? Something that stands head and shoulders above the competition. A shining example of going above and beyond. Hors categorie[124]. Or as Rufus, Cooter and Skeeter[125] would say, "Oooooowee! Thet's wa-a-ay better then I kin do!" I couldn't have said it better myself. (BTW: R, C & S have almost saved up enough to get a complete set of 23 chromosomes… between them. Where there's life, there's hope.)

Excellence manifests itself in many ways; a particularly close adherence to demanding tolerances on a consistent basis (think NASA joint efforts with Space-X,) particularly high ratings in relation to others in academic pursuits (Magna Cum Laude, Valedictorian,) intellectual acumen (Chess Grand Master, MIT Think Tank,) building a happy, healthy and balanced family (my family put the "fun" in dysfunctional,) athletics (Heisman Trophy Winner, MVP, Super Bowl winners, Olympic medalists) the list is endless.

excellence

Wherever there is a statistical mean or a preponderance of mediocrity, there is an obvious place for excellence.

Since nature abhors a vacuum, the void literally sucks overachievers into that space. They can't help it. It's an inexorable force of nature. Like touching something marked, "Wet Paint," or a four year-old confronted with a tantalizingly icky, mud puddle while wearing a tiny, perfectly color-coordinated and rented ("Nothing parties like a rental!"[126]) tuxedo just moments before the processional begins to play, or a galaxy-class, black hole (much akin to my 10th grade Algebra II class.) "Resistance is futile.[127]" Or is it?

The Borg Queen never assimilated Freddie Mercury.

Well, if it really was futile, there would be no reason for this book. I would just write a book entitled, "Nothing to see here. Move along." But I didn't. And won't. There's lots to see here and it's all obvious. Perhaps the most obvious thing is: People can change. And

the obvious path

excellence

that includes – you. So resist the common paradigm and its associated corollaries. Stick to the obvious. But, it will require thought. Lots of it. Clear thought. Unencumbered thought. Once you decide to become obvious, you will never be able to "just accept what they say anymore." "They" have lost sight of the real truth. The unequivocal, singular absolute truth that is so obvious that it hurts not to express it. Your job becomes to perceive it, test it, prove it, accept it, internalize it, apply it, express it and live it. It's a process. You will never completely assimilate it or express it. It will take your entire life to live it. And ultimately, your life will be a book to those who follow. Even if it's just one person, for one generation.

Think about your legacy for a moment. What kind of legacy will you leave? Let me start with a few questions. What does your great-grandfather's breath smell like? What was your grandmother's favorite ice cream? What is your third uncle's middle name? What was the most relevant concept your father learned in middle school? If you can't answer these questions, don't feel bad. Most people can't. The point is: What do we really know about our ancestors? How far back?

excellence

How much is verifiable?
What is their legacy?

Truth be known, our legacy doesn't survive the generations unless it is a concept or idea. Concepts and ideas don't have a shelf-life. They are eternal (for lack of a better word.) But just as a simple sentence can become something totally unrecognizable in a game of "Jungle Telephone[128]," so can ideas and concepts. If it is true that, "History is written by the victors[129]," then those who propagate and perpetuate the concepts and ideas will "personalize" the message as it is passed along. Where is the certitude of the message? Where is the integrity of the legacy? Now before you go and draw a warm bath, pour a glass of vintage wine and open a vein is anguished despair over the irrelevance of your life and its legacy, pause a moment (or ten or twelve.) Your legacy is obvious.

Ahhh, that struck a chord. Imagine if you will, that you truly

the obvious path

do have a legacy well worth passing down to future generations. What is the best way to preserve the essence of it throughout all future transmissions? Simple. Make it obvious – AND – teach the benefactor of it to internalize and live the precepts of being obvious, while teaching the next recipient to do the same. "If you give a man a fish, he won't be hungry for a day. If you teach him to fish, he will feed himself for a lifetime." Share your obviosity. It won't diminish in the giving away of it, but will actually increase in the giving.

"If you want something, give it away."

The obvious key to abundance is for everybody to share. Then everybody has an abundance. But, the moment someone withholds, even to the slightest degree, the cycle begins to contract. It gains exponential momentum until all sharing stops and collapse begins. It is the surest and fastest path to want and poverty. Then comes oppression and ultimately total destruction.

> Abundance can't be legislated into existence. It can only be created through voluntary sharing.

"Why not just hold everybody accountable to share?" Obviously the answer is the overwhelming preponderance of evidence against that proposal. You simply can't legislate morality. It has never worked to date and there is no reason that it will ever will (refer to Uncle Al's definition of insanity.)

No. Sharing begets abundance when the people understand its obviosity and internalize it as their own paradigm. Alexis de Tocqueville[130], a French political scientist, philosopher and historian once said, "America is great, because America is good. If America ever ceases being good, America will cease to be great." The nexus of his premise is the notion of an internal, moral clock – goodness. Our founding fathers knew that the Constitution would be unworkable if the citizens ever lacked deeply held, positive personal values. Legislating morality is by nature totally unenforceable as a means to enforce "goodness." So much for the Civics lesson.

Deeply embedded internal values drive the character of any group or organization.

"So how do we get people to share?" Obvious. We share. And teach others to do the same thing. If this understanding abundance of the Sharing Economy is inextricably intertwined with the legacy we intend to pass down, we have installed the mechanics for its unending existence and the same for abundance. At that point, does it really matter if the inceptor of the legacy is known by name? Your legacy has lived on. Isn't that the point? Consider any historical figure you can think of for a moment. Were they really that way you "know" or "remember" them. Very doubtful. Did

excellence

Rolls[131] get along with Royce[132]? Did Marie Antoinette[133] excoriate[134], eructate[135] and flatulate[136] in midst of the French court? Did Washington really never tell a lie? Did Al Gore really invent the internet? We'll probably never know. That's the point. Almost certainly, historical profiles do not accurately encompass the essence of the real figure. The teller colors the tale.

So, if we pursue excellence as the basis for leaving a legacy, at what cost do we press the chase? Obviously, excellence is pursued to the exclusion of other, lesser objectives. One cannot be excellent at everything. To excel, one must specialize and focus as on a singularity. There's only so much of you to go around. So, you must focus on the thing in which you intend to excel. Sounds pretty straightforward, doesn't it? One might say it's obvious. That's only because it is.

How will you balance your excellence?

"But, what about the people who excel at a buncha' stuff?" Well, I just read about a guy[137] that was a Navy SEAL[138], a Harvard Doctor and a NASA Astronaut. I know that SEALs maintain a super-high level of readiness (physical, mental, emotional, warfighter skills) and have developed their team orientation to the maximum. A Harvard educated doctor enters the curriculum at the top of the pack and

excellence

develops not only the skills but application of those same skills to the highest levels. Astronauts are not only the best of the best when it comes to applicable skills, but they have also been exhaustively vetted for their psychological readiness to execute their role. Classic example of the super overachiever.

"Yeah, but you said excellence is achieved at the expense of the other areas in one's life."

Yes, I did. I'm glad you were paying attention. But, what is obvious is that these areas of excellence were not all achieved concurrently. I guarantee that when our super overachiever was going through BUDs[139] training, he gave no thought or energy to becoming a Harvard trained doctor. And, when he was in Harvard writing his doctoral thesis he gave no attention to becoming an astronaut. I guarantee he gave all of his attention to each task at hand. His achievements were attained consecutively, not concurrently. I'm not privy to the other areas in his life, but necessarily they must have taken second fiddle to his primary objective. Contrary to popular belief, men cannot multi-task. That is the sole domain of moms and effective women in general. Men think in boxes. Women think in spaghetti. (No invective–laced emails or doxxing, please. Women are just better at certain things than men.)

Obviously, some things suffered while he was single-mindedly pursuing each area of excellence. Maintenance is a different story. He obviously maintains his physical conditioning for his

excellence

astronaut duties. He obviously maintains his doctoral credentials and continues to learn and apply new skills as an astronaut. I don't know, but I would imagine he focuses on whatever goal is in front of him with laser-like singularity until he achieves his goal. Perhaps that focus and application is his singular area of excellence. I don't know. But, I do know that he puts on his pants one leg at a time, unlike Ozzie Nelson[140].

I think the imbalanced nature of excellence is becoming clearer to you now. Focus is the key. Focus is exclusive by nature. I have been accused of having laser-like focus. Especially by my wife when I'm watching TV. Or maybe it's just a guy thing. (Again, no nastygrams, please. Men do one thing at a time. Sometimes we look like we're multi-tasking, but we're actually just switching very rapidly from one task to another, much like alternating current. Or ADD. It's a constraint, but it also has an upside. Focus.) So, we beg the question: "Is focus (to the exclusion of all else) bad?" As with all double-edged swords, no. It just comes with a specialized set of criteria. Use the right tool for the right job. Extreme specialization may be good for a doctor in a burgeoning field of general practitioners, but not so much as a "simple country doctor[141]." The country doctor will be called upon to deal with everything from a hand snagged into a hay baler, to Aunt Tillie "feelin' kinda' puny," to acute

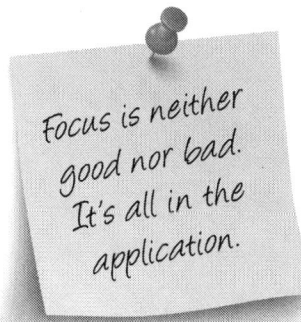

Focus is neither good nor bad. It's all in the application.

tachycardia[142] with a compromised thymoglobulin[143] level. A neuroendocrinological radioncologist[144] may be sorely pressed to deal with little Timmy's dislocated pinkie. There's a place for generalists and a place for specialists. They rarely overlap.

At the risk of continuing to inflict egregious, blunt-force trauma on an Equus Ferus Caballus that has assumed ambient temperature[145], while excellence arises from imbalance, it is not necessarily a bad thing. One of the biggest drawbacks is that excellence tends to place the person on a pedestal because of their excellence. Now a pedestal is a beautiful thing to behold. It presents the object of adulation in an elevated manner that separates it from the surrounding environment. Generally the platform at the top of the pedestal is barely big enough to showcase the featured article's base. Should that featured article be a person, the top of the pedestal barely accommodates their feet. Herein lies the rub. For the person to step in any direction, irrespective of the goodness of their intentions, results in a clear and specific proof of gravity. (read: "Watch that first step. It's a biggie.") So herein lies the conundrum[146]: "Any movement, with the exception of vertically results in a sudden and precipitous drop." There's those pesky Laws of Physics, again. To continue to rise vertically in order to stay on top of the pedestal requires exponentially greater

Pedestals are dangerous places.

focus and effort. Being finite beings, we soon discover that this plan of action is ultimately unsustainable. So, refocus or fall. Even as in the case of our friend the SEAL/Dr./Astronaut, there must necessarily be at least a small retraction in stature when transitioning to a parallel area of discipline. He didn't muster out of the SEALs on Monday, become a Harvard doctor on Tuesday and then an Astronaut on Wednesday. Even if he did, the mornings would be a little lower than the afternoons and he would need to transition overnight to the next area of endeavor. It would not be a steady increase from Monday to Thursday.

Now, let's discuss the Halo Effect[147]. As you can imagine from the name, it involves having the appearance of an angel. Dangerous perception. Especially, if you're a mere mortal. The effect kinda' goes like this: "If you're a really good (fill-in-the-blank) employee, you'll most certainly be an excellent (fill-in-the-blank) manager." I'm sure we've all worked with someone who got booted upstairs. The poor individual was really good at their job. They loved what they did. Management was exceptionally pleased with their attitude and their performance. All their co-workers loved them. And suddenly, they're the Boss. Entirely different set of skills. Sure they knew their area of expertise backwards and forward. But, people skills? Mmmm... Not so much. Management training? Prolly not. Just super-high expectations (because of their excellent performance) and a whole lot of pressure. "Surely, they'll be an outstanding (fill-in-the-blank) manager.

The sky's the limit for them!" Kiss of death. Two periods later while they are careening in flames toward the earth, generally hating life and probably collapsing in their personal life, everybody is dumbfounded. "How could this happen? They were such a good (fill-in-the-blank). So sad. Meanwhile this person can only wish they could go back to being a totally happy and fulfilled (fill-in-the-blank). This process can often be more protracted (and consequently much more painful) as they keep getting booted upstairs. "Surely they'll do better next time…" This continues until they reach their level of total incompetence. Larry[148] explores this phenomenon in his eponymously[149] titled book called "The Peter Principle." No wonder the C-level is often populated with tap-dancing hacks. Not good for anybody, including the company. Grow where you're planted. Unless you're a vine and designed for the upward mobility in the corporate world, you may fall victim to the Halo Effect until you top out in soul-crushing incompetence.

So, strangely enough, excellence, and the singular imbalance therein, may actually be setting you up for failure. "No-o-o-o-o-o… Say it isn't so!" Sorry, it's just obvious. The good news is that excellence can be balanced. "Wait a minute! You said excellence arises out of imbalance! Now you're saying you can have excellence and balance!? What gives? "You got some 'splainin' to do, Ricky![150]"

OK. Here it is. Don't co-locate all your ovum in a solitary,

excellence

woven carry receptacle. ("Don't put all your eggs in one basket." See, I just saved you a trip to the "What the heck did he just say…?" Section. Nice Guy, huh? I have my moments.) Or as your financial adviser would say, "Diversify your portfolio based on your risk tolerance[151]." When you're young you can afford to pursue excellence with a singular focus and passion. If you crash and burn, you can get up and do it again. (Hopefully without the crash and burn part…) As you progress in your career you will want to broaden your areas of expertise and experience so that you can migrate the creative principles horizontally to other areas that you're good at and would like to be. Nothing sucks worse than being in a job that you hate but need to support your habit of living indoors and taking regular meals. Creative principles are obviously interchangeable between all the various areas of creative expression. Be sure to step back far enough to recognize the obvious principles and how to re-purpose them. Don't be a one-trick pony[152] 'cause when the circus leaves town, you'll be left high and dry. And that sux.

Oscar Wilde[153] once penned, "Everything in moderation, including moderation." Sam Clemens[154] put it in context of his enjoyment of adult beverages, "Temperant temperance is best. Intemperant temperance is troublesome." That balance can be achieved by living the obvious lifestyle. But, more on that later.

Have other things you can do well and develop them concurrently with the singular thing that you excel at. You won't go as high as in that singular, excellent area. But then again, you won't fall as far to one of the other areas you have nurtured and grown. Have a backup plan. And have a backup plan for your backup plan. As "Ol' Blood and Guts[155]" once famously said, "Plan A goes out the window as soon as the first shot is fired." Do you really want to only have a Plan A in your life?

"So, it seems you're speaking against excellence in favor of a moderated balance." Not so. Obviously, excellence is defined by where and how you choose to pursue it. You may choose to excel in balance. With that comes stability. Stability can be just another form of excellence. It is not necessarily a denomination of mediocrity or bland, uninspired uniformity. If you want that, just stay where you are and avoid the obvious at all costs. If that's not what you want, pursue the obvious in terms of your own creative genius and bring that to the marketplace of humanity in newness of life. Share it with others and teach them how to replicate the process. Now you have a legacy that they can and will build on as a common legacy to the benefit of all who encounter it. Who cares if your name is on it? Isn't the legacy

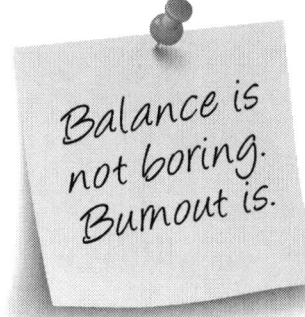

Balance is not boring. Burnout is.

the whole point? Obviously, yes.

Your creative genius will express itself wherever you allow and direct it to go. It is going all the time. It's gonna' go somewhere. It might as well be where you want it to go.

> *Your creative genius will be expressed.*

My, my. Now isn't that empowering. I get to determine where my creativity will manifest in the direction and to the degree I desire. Keep in mind that with that comes a huge responsibility for the application. The outcome is not in your control. It only seems so in concurrence with happenstance[156] and serendipity[157]. See, I told you this wasn't some rah-rah, PMA book that tells you, "Anything you can conceive and believe, you can achieve." "Name it and claim it." "Blab it and grab it."

Not so. Great things happen in community. When people see you operating effectively in your creativity, they are obviously drawn to join in with you and your apparent success. When you show them how to manifest their own creativity, they obviously see the multiplier effect of the joint effort and help you see the obvious direction and goal of your combined creative energies. The application is your responsibility, however the outcome is not. See the obvious things that are too big for one person to do, then show others how to see their obvious creativity. Then show them how to tap into it and then finally, manifest it in ways that are bigger than they are. The results will obviously be beyond your expectations and imagination.

That, my fellow obvious friend, is excellence from balance.

obvious excellence CHECKLIST

- [ ] Excellence comes in many forms, but is always superior in quality.
- [ ] What cost are you willing to pay for it?
- [ ] Excellence comes from imbalance.
- [ ] Pedestals are dangerous places.
- [ ] Your Halo is often a setup for failure.
- [ ] Excellence from balance is better.

notes:

chap 7

"Cogni... what?"

Cognitive Dissonance. Get used to it. You will be experiencing it more and more as you start living the obvious lifestyle. But, there's a significant difference between classical cognitive dissonance and the one you will feel.

In 1957, Psychologist Leon Festinger[158] first noted the existence of the psychological tension he named "Cognitive Dissonance." He described it as the uneasy feeling a person gets when their behavior doesn't match a closely held, personal belief. He also postulated that people would work very hard to maintain their original paradigm, especially in light of contraindicative information. For example, let's say a person is known to be very frugal and they think of themselves in the same way. It's a value they hold in high esteem and identify with it as being part and parcel of who they are. Now, let's say they make a truly extravagant purchase. Let's say a Classic Rolex Presidential with the Diamond Bezel[159]. They've never owned anything more extravagant than a Casio G-Force[160], so this is a definitive departure from their previous buying habits. People notice. They notice. The watch seems to weigh even heavier on their psyche than on their wrist (which is saying a lot. Those dang things are heavy...) So now there is a dynamic tension living within the person as this totally out of character purchase conflicts with their dearly held paradigm of frugality. What's a Mother to do[161]?

Well, reconciliation comes in many forms. Denial is popular (which is NOT a river in Egypt, as Bill's friends[162] often say.) "This purchase IS frugal. It will only increase in value so it's a good investment." The same self-delusion is shared by the guy who just bought that bright, shiny, "Arrest Me Red" Corvette from the corner of the lot. Nobody really buys their story, but the denier must reconcile the dissonance or live in a constant state of being unsettled. No rest for the wicked.

"So, how is that accomplished?" you ask. For the answer to that question may I refer you to your Freshman Class in "Rationalization 101." Your creative genius kicks into overdrive and you come up with a bazillion plausible reasons why you bought that Rolex. Anything to absolve yourself of the guilt of violating one of your own, foundational, personal beliefs. And either you find a suitable excuse, or you must confront your antithetical behavior and take steps to mitigate the situation.

Please understand that all decisions are emotional. They come

the obvious path

dissonance

from the right side of the brain. The same place where your creativity comes from. It's a delightful place. I spend much, if not most of my time there. It's the place where everything is possible and I get to control all the crayons in the BIG box[163] (the one with the built-in sharpener in the back!) That's where we see the pictures in the clouds, feel the emotions of the moment, delight in beauty, surge in lust (Hey! How did that get in there!?) And we all make our decisions there. "But, wait!" you protest. "What about technical decisions and rational decisions? Hmmmm…?"

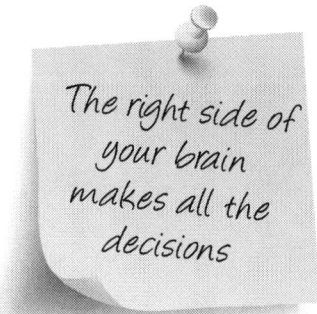

Well, what about 'em? Decisions are all forced by a moral dilemma. Once you are aware of the existence of two, mutually exclusive directions you can take, you must resolve the paradox. It is a moral imperative. You simply must choose. There is no alternative. The misconception comes in here about which side of the brain is the initiator of the decision. If a so-called "rational" choice is made, it's easy to assume the left brain made the decision.

When in fact, the left brain only became involved once the decision was made by the right brain and was called upon to list all the good reasons the decision was made. ("Yes, buying that red Corvette was a good decision, because (fill-in-the-blank-rationalization...) Those reasons all align with a person's closely held personal paradigms. To make a decision that violates those paradigms creates cognitive dissonance and once again, the person is confronted with a decision that must be made. One way or another, you're going to have to make a decision that aligns with your personal value structure or be thrust into an arena of psychological tension – "uneasiness." That need for resolution is an incredibly powerful motivator. If not resolved, the consequences can be just as powerfully paralyzing and ultimately destructive. Fade to black. ("Man, this guy just keeps getting dark, doesn't he?") Not really. You don't have to go there. You just have to see what is obvious and act accordingly – in alignment with your personal paradigms. Simple, just not always easy. Oh, well. Welcome to life.

But, humans are not altruistic beings. They will only do what is best for themselves. "But wait!" You cry. "What about the guy who throws himself on the hand grenade to save his buddies? Surely, that's not in his best interest. That's in the best interest of his buddies!"

Certainly seems that way, doesn't it? But let's take a closer look.

First, what is altruism? Merriam-Webster[164] has it as:

> *"1: unselfish regard for or devotion to the welfare of others, charitable acts motivated purely by altruism.*
>
> *2: behavior by an animal that is not beneficial to or may be harmful to itself but that benefits others of its species."*

Seems like a slam-dunk, doesn't it? Perhaps...

But, is it really the obvious perspective? Let's back up and start at the beginning. Is humankind really foundationally and fundamentally good? Empirically, no. Statistically, no. Genealogically, no. Intrinsically, no. Physiologically, not any more than any other animal. Socially, no. Politically, no. How long must I go on...?

"OK. But there are so many things humankind has done that ARE good. How could that be if humankind is not fundamentally good?"

Let's not confuse behavior with being. Hitler was sincerely kind and genuinely caring toward his secretaries. Ted Bundy[165] was a really "nice guy" to his landlady. John Wayne Gacey[166] regularly brought joy to children's hospitals and charitable events as "Pogo the Clown." He was also active in his local community as a political party precinct captain, deeply concerned with the benefit and well-being of his neighbors. Wonderful, kind and loving behavior. Not essence of being.

"Oh, yeah... well you still haven't addressed the guy who throws himself on the hand grenade to save his buddies? That's not in his best interest, now is it?"

Well, in actual fact, it is. (Enter: Enlightened Self-interest[167]; Cue SFX: Heavenly chorale and ethereal shaft of light; Audio fade to Narrator.)

Humankind is hard-wired to do what is best for themselves. It's a survival instinct. Momentarily setting aside the discussion of morality, let's look at the illusion of altruism. A person can have a foundational paradigm that states the well-being of their family, or comrades at arms, is superior to the well-being of the individual – including their own. To violate that paradigm is totally incongruent with their self-image to the extent that it must be avoided at all costs, even one's own life. So, it is in their best self-interest as a human being to jump on that hand grenade and save the lives of their unit in combat, because the alternative is unthinkable. They could never live with themselves if they took the coward's way out and leaped to their own safety, while subsequently allowing their brothers to die in a horrible explosion. In the cold, clear light of reason, remaining consistent with one's paradigm is in one's own best interest as the alternative is unthinkable. That's enlightened self-interest.

However, the decision remains emotional and the rationalization and justification for the decision is still made by the left brain – even though the decision seems ostensibly logical in that it is made to support one's foundational paradigm. That sounds logical, right?

The original decision to adopt the foundational paradigm was made because it was "good" (insert your own definition of "good" here) as a consistent code of behavior.)

("Golly, he keeps getting serious. It's making my head hurt.")

Well, decisions are serious business, and when made following the obvious course of action, they produce wonderful and beneficial results – for everyone involved. Let's move on.

The other tack you can take is confrontation. This is by far the more difficult approach, but certainly the most authentic. Sometimes you just have to take the bull by the tail and face the situation. Once you sincerely and forthrightly face the situation you have any number of options at your disposal. You could return the Rolex, or sell it. You could keep the watch and simply acknowledge that you just want it, with no need for explanation, irrespective of its outlier status among your hallowed, self-defining, life paradigms. Just keep the dang thing and enjoy it. The watch has no right or wrong attached to it. You obviously just need to resolve it in your own heart. It's just a thing.

You can also choose to just accept the ongoing contradiction as normal. Not quite the same thing as denial, but certainly just as insipid in its application. Remember, one cannot spend any protracted time in a state of irresolution. It will pop out in your

dissonance

life at some remarkably inappropriate time and in some mind boggling manner. Overreactions. "Acting out." Disappearing. Blurting out Tourette's[168]-like utterances to the boss' husband at the Annual Picnic. It's gonna' come out somehow. You can't keep a foundational contradiction bottled up and act like you've accepted it as normal. Your head will explode.

Another, more viable option is to do the courageous work of changing your paradigm. It can be done. People change. However, everybody says they want change, but nobody actually wants to do it. Years of project management and change management have taught me that little nugget. Change simply forces them out of their comfort zone. Nobody likes 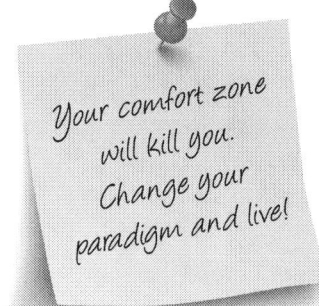 that, even the people that do it and as a result become wildly successful. (You should write that down or something…) Never forget: Your comfort zone will kill you. Slowly. The converse of that equation is to change your offending behavior. Then again, that involves that pesky "change thing." Hmmm… "I guess this set of options all involve change." Yup. Something's gotta' give. You don't have to go home, but you can't stay here[169].

On the other hand (besides the four fingers and the thumb, assuming you started with that configuration, unlike my friend Mark[170] who delights in springing "hand jokes" on unsuspecting people he meets.) are moral decisions involving life and death,

dissonance

yours or someone else's. This really kicks it up to a whole 'nother order of magnitude, Bubba (or Bubbette, whichever the case may be.) At this point, your sense of morality, "goodness" grandly steps onto center stage with great aplomb. This decision directly impacts your concept of who you really are. No place for unresolved cognitive dissonance here. No, you are now confronted with a decision you absolutely must make, or it will literally and certifiably drive you insane (for some of us it's a shorter drive than others.) Isn't life grand?

An even worse option is known as adopting the "normalcy bias[171]." It is defined as a state where a person fails to recognize the danger in front of them and continues forward as if "everything's going to be fine." "It will all return to normal" [*Ed. Note: "Normal" is just a setting on your dryer.*] This is a very dangerous place to be. You are not listening to your creative genius and missing everything that is being made so very obvious to you. Wishing doesn't make it so. This is also known as the "Brown Zone." (Refer to Chapter 3, "Oblivious to the Obvious") It's a place you never want to be. "If it looks like a duck, and quacks like a duck and walks like a duck, there's a very strong probability that it is, in fact, an Anas[172]– or at least something in the same Genus." You've heard people say, "Go with your gut." Or you're in a situation where things "just don't add up." That's because they don't! Trust your instincts! Now, get outta' there! As fast as you can. "Run Forrest, run![173]"

But, fear not. All is not lost. Just step back and take a look at what's obvious in this situation. You will see it. Loud and clear (to mix a metaphor…) It will stare you in the face. Not with intimidation and anger, but with love and dispassionate reality. This is where you need to trust your creative genius to softly whisper the best possible course to take, without judgment or coercion. Just look and see. It's uniquely obvious… to you. That's the beauty.

> *Trust your creative genius to advise you in a way that is totally unique to you.*

But, you must trust your creative genius. It will whisper in the good times and shout in your pain. It is always there. It will never leave you hangin'. If you have any doubts, reread the chapter on Trust. But, first you must understand there's a difference between trust and belief.

Have you ever gotten your car up to 70 MPH on the highway? (Some of you on a back road… or your driveway) You did that out of trust. You trusted that your brakes could bring you back down to 0 MPH in a safe and controlled manner. Otherwise you never would have taken the car up to 70 MPH in the first place. You're not stoopid. Right? OK, so now you see your exit coming up ahead. It's time to act like you really believe your brakes are going to do what you trusted them to do. At the exact micro-instant that you decide to lift your foot off the accelerator and put it on the brake – but, BEFORE you even send the electrical impulse down your leg to initiate the action, is belief. The belief that necessarily demands an action. Belief is not like watching Peter Pan[174] and believing that if you want it bad enough and clap your hands long enough and loud enough, that Tinker Bell[175] will live. Nope. That's wishful thinking. Belief is putting your money where your mouth is. Belief is acting like what you believe is true. There is no such thing as blind faith. So-called "blind faith" is the domain of fools. Real faith is much more serious and much more powerful than that. But, it must be based on trust. It is the space where the obvious is made manifest. Where it becomes real.

It takes courage, my friend. It takes wisdom. It takes understanding and finally, it takes knowledge. The truth is always obvious. It's made that way. Trust it.

But, I'm not talking about classical cognitive dissonance here, I'm talking about the flip side[176] of cognitive dissonance. The dark side of CD. The alter ego. The "evil twin." I'm talking about when you see it out in the wild and it tempts you to reconcile it according to your own personal, moral paradigms. This happens a lot with magicians and politicians. Of course, magicians merely do it to entertain you, but politicians do it for power and control. This is where magicians and politicians have a great deal in common. But the good news is, it's easy to tell when they are creating it in you.

Cognitive dissonance has a dark side.

Their lips are moving.

Pretty obvious, eh? Yes, it is. A magician will be talking and misdirecting your thoughts and attention to someplace other than where the actual "switcheroo" is being made. As anyone who has ever seriously practiced the martial arts will tell you, the moment of transition is the most vulnerable. So, if you misdirect your opponent's attention to someplace other than the awareness of the transition, you maintain the illusion and press on to strength. A politician will press on to the public perception that they are "stupid." "Man, I can't believe how stupid (fill-in-the-blank) politician is. Look how (wrong/damaging/counter-intuitive/antithetical/etc.) that new policy/law is! They must be totally stupid!!"

Not so. I will posit here that there's not a stupid politician on the planet. They didn't get where they are by being stupid. They got there by misdirection. All worldly governance is by deception and misdirection. Otherwise how could so few control so many? Juvenal[177] noticed this back in the first century C.E. when he said, "Panem et circenses[178]" (bread and circuses) he was referring to placating the general populace by supplying their physical needs (bread) and their diversions from what is actually happening (circuses.) Quite effective, actually. Cicero[179] even noted, "The evil was not in panem et circenses, per se, but in the willingness of the people to sell their rights as free men for full bellies and the excitement of the games which would serve to distract them from the other human hungers which bread and circuses can never appease.[180]" Bazinga![181] The old double–whammy: External manipulation and baser human nature. As a precaution, any martial artist will tell you, "Never listen to what your opponent is saying, always watch their hands. Hands kill." Words to live by. Whatever they are doing is what they intended to do. What they wanted to do. They're not stupid.

There is not a single stupid politician on the planet

But here's the catch: We as moral, rational, kind and reasonable human beings can't conceive of the evil (…there's that word. Can't have "good" without "evil") intentions or outcome of the behavior we are witnessing so we must reconcile this cognitive dissonance and the only resolution we can "reasonably" come up with is; "They must be stupid." Not only is that complete denial, but it is dangerous. Deadly dangerous.

So, let's back away from the precipice for a moment, shall we? You obviously don't have to step off that cliff. It's like the moment Beau Geste[182] marches, blindfolded to the very edge of certain death and at the absolutely last possible moment, his Commander screams, "Halt!" Beau stops and then is commanded to remove his blindfold only to see how close he came to a horrific demise, and nearly falls forward at the realization as he is irresistibly drawn into the void. His Commander steadies him and draws him back from the edge, unharmed. His trust and belief rescued him from overwhelmingly horrible consequences. All because of his trust and belief. Trust in his Commander's orders as being in his best interests and belief to act accordingly.

Your creative genius will always alert you when you are succumbing to external cognitive dissonance. You simply need to obey that little voice and act accordingly. If it doesn't seem right, it probably isn't. But, once you open your eyes and realize how close you came to bad consequences, your creative genius will lead you gently back from the edge. Then in that moment, you finally understand the wisdom of listening to the obvious from your creative genius, and acting responsively upon that wisdom. Or ignore the warning and march headlong into the void.

People who seek to use/abuse you are not stupid, but they are obvious. Don't listen to what they say. Watch their hands. Actions kill, not words. Now aren't you glad you have a creative genius in your everyday life that is more than willing and very eager to show you the obvious? The obvious is always there – in plain sight. You can see it, but are you willing to heed its wisdom and act accordingly on it? If not, there are people just waiting out there that not only want to hurt you and practice how to do it, but they enjoy doing it. Don't be stupid. Be obvious.

Well, I think by now we have firmly established that Cognitive Dissonance is actually your friend. It is a distant, early warning system emanating from your subconscious, and luckily for you, your subconscious never sleeps. The challenge is: To hear that small voice among all the clutter that is your life. That clutter can be physical noise, or emotional distraction, pain in whatever form, visual complexity, intentional inattention or any of the other myriad things that vie for our attention on a regular and ongoing basis, all day, every day. Marketers thrive on finding new ways to "break through the clutter," to motivate you to manifest the desired behavior; grab your TOMA[183] (Top of Mind Awareness), change brand preference or reinforce brand preference – read: "Buy something." Your toddler or your teen simply must have your full attention when you are either on the throne or on the phone. Everyone and everything wants your attention. It's a lot of noise. Some people count on that noise. They hope it masks their intentions or hides their actions. Still others just add to it, "Because they can." It's a relentless onslaught to impact you, your life and your decisions. Other than becoming an ascetic monk in some obscure religious sect, secluded high up on a lofty crag in the Himalayas, what should you do? The obvious. No matter how far or fast you run, your problems and clutter will follow you. Just stop. See what's in front of you. Exhale. Listen to your creative genius. Take a deep breath. And do. The obvious.

> Obviosity cuts through the noise.

obvious dissonance CHECKLIST

- [ ] There's a difference between internal and external cognitive dissonance.
- [ ] Cognitive dissonance must be reconciled or your head will explode.
- [ ] There are numerous ways to resolve it, pick one.
- [ ] The Normalcy Bias = Brown Zone.
- [ ] Trust and belief in your creative genius is mission critical.
- [ ] Cognitive Dissonance is your friend.

notes:

chap 8

Obviously Toxic

We have all worked with them. Perhaps you grew up with some. Maybe they were in your family. Maybe it's you. But toxic people are everywhere. They're in your life... for a purpose.

Oh, they could be the sweet, well-meaning Aunt who is never satisfied with what her "favorite niece/nephew" has accomplished. Perhaps they are the gatekeeper to your next promotion. Maybe they're a salesperson to whom you are required to provide creative support wrenched from your gut on a daily basis. Or it could be that face in the mirror. They're all toxic. Poison. To anyone and anything that enters their domain. Without going into all their personal and psychological issues at this point, let me just reiterate that, "Hurt people, hurt people." No, that is not a repetitive admonition to go out and hurt people. It simply means that people who have been hurt (which includes ALL of us) tend to want to displace that pain to someone else, "So they know what it feels like." Childish? Yes. Human? Yes.

It reminds me of a story (most things do...) I was in junior high and desperately wanting to discover my identity. The lunchroom was the crucible of all things pubescent. Everybody was there. From the "cool kids" (who really weren't) to the Hoods (read:

Thugs,) the Jocks, the Cheerleaders, the Nerds (long before it was cool,) the Smart Kids, the Doofae (I think that's the plural of "doofus," I'm not sure,) the Greasers (pre-cursor to "Motorheads",) the Hippies, the Wallflowers, the Artsy-Fartsy Types, the "Band Club", the "Choir/Drama" Queens, the Loners, and the rest of us great, unwashed masses. (My apologies if I've left out your particular or favorite tribe among the hyper-hormonal[184] throngs of Middle School humanity.) For myself, I really didn't fit in anywhere, but moved among the tribes pretty easily. Especially in the lunchroom.

One day, as the story goes, I had just trans-navigated the gauntlet of the steam table between me and all the scary people with hairnets and rubber gloves dishing up supposedly edible stuff on our trays. Today was Tuesday, so we had a chocolate cream pie substitute for dessert. I say "substitute" because it appeared to be industrial chocolate pudding dumped into a pre-made pie crust with something vaguely resembling Cool Whip[186], or a derivative,

"Trust the pie."[185]

the obvious path

© 2021 Elephantine Press, LLC

spread on top. This little triangle of culinary pretension sat on the melamine plate looking very lonely but glad to escape the uniform confines of the cafeteria line. I got my little container of chocolate milk and headed out into the vast

A middle school lunchroom is a microcosm of life.

wilderness before me. There, to my surprise, was an open seat across from someone I kinda' knew at one of the endless picnic tables that populated the insanely cavernous lunchroom. So, I plopped down and said, "Hi!" The person across from me looked up and hovered his hand over my slice of pseudo-chocolate confection and said, "Wow! His pie is hot, too!" Quite taken aback by this otherworldly observation of the exothermal[187] properties of my dessert, I hovered my hand over the slice to confirm his postulation[188]. At which point, he deftly pressed my hand down into the gooey glop masquerading as my pie and burst into uncontrollable, early-teen laughter. After he and his friends all caught their breath, they got up and left me there with pie on my hand. (I guess in retrospect it was better than having pie on my face.) But wait. There's more…

I was now filled with the indomitable and overwhelmingly immediate necessity to "Pass it along." I waited patiently for my quarry to fill the seat across the table from me. Soon my patience was rewarded with fresh meat. An unsuspecting schlemozzel[189] had taken their place across from me with a fresh piece of quasi-chocolate cream pie on his tray. I quizzically extended my palm over his pie and exclaimed, "Wow! His pie is hot, too!" Then, exactly as I had anticipated, the poor schnook[190] put his hand over his pie. My moment of exquisite retribution had arrived in all of its pseudo-pastry glory. I raised my hand over his pie while making a fist and came down on the target with malice of forethought and extreme focus. Not to mention, "really hard and fast." What I hadn't anticipated was the speed of his reflexes. He deftly pulled his hand out of the path of my gloriously impending fist at the last possible nano-moment. My fist came down directly on the epi-center of his chocolate cream pie with authority and power. I was suddenly overtaken with uncontrollable, teenage laughter, (which was not shared by anyone else in the blast radius) and room temperature, gloppy, brown detritus. Some things have a way of going sideways in the most entertaining fashion.

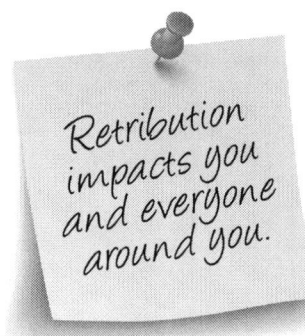
Retribution impacts you and everyone around you.

Hurt people, hurt people.

Now, carry that same behavior forward into adult life and the stakes become exponentially higher. Life is written in ink and so is the pain. One can choose to process the pain in an emotionally intelligent[191] way, or simply revert to teenage solutions and "pass it along." You may not even realize you are passing it along. It may seem quite normal and invisible to you. I assure you, it is not. This response to pain stimuli is now toxic. To you and everybody who encounters it.

It's like unforgiveness. Unforgiveness is where you drink the poison and wait for the other person to die. It eats at you. It makes you as ugly as the portrait in Dorian Gray's attic[192]. Other people sense it in you. On you. They get splashed by your overflow. And all the while, you have no idea of the effect you're having on yourself and those around you. Everybody except the person you haven't forgiven. They probably have no idea that any of this is going on and are happily going on with their life, unencumbered by the poison coursing through your veins. Yuck! Just stop it. You've become toxic simply because you have chosen not to forgive someone.

Forgiveness is not endorsing. It is liberating.

Forgiveness does NOT mean endorsing the behavior that you need to forgive. Nor does it mean you have to place yourself in the same position again that caused you to receive the offending behavior in the first place. It means that you simply let it go, and move on. "But, I can't do that! You don't know what they did to me!" No I don't. But that's not the point. It's not about me, it's about you. It's not about them, it's about you. You can change the situation. You can make the choice to relegate it to the past; a place you can't change and focus on going forward. Obviously, we only have the now. Live in its obviosity.

"Forgiveness is the fragrance the violet leaves on the heel that crushed it," says old Sam Clemens[193]. Far more healthy and effective than revenge.

Kinda' sounds like cycles, doesn't it? Well, that's because it is. The good thing about cycles is, they can be broken. But, only if you want to. Alcoholics have to "hit bottom." Smokers have to "want to quit." Us "Fluffy-types" have to really believe, "Nothing tastes as good as skinny feels." (I'm not there, yet. But, I'm headed that direction out of a sense of self-preservation.) You gotta' wanna' break the cycle. Period. All else will end in dismal and eventually soul-crushing failure. Oh, goody. More pain.

OK. So you get the obvious point here. It's a cycle. Cycles are predictable. So are toxic people. "So, why can't I deal with them since they're so obviously toxic? I mean I have to deal with this jerk every single day. What can I do without going to prison for the rest of my natural life?" There are a myriad of answers to that question, but they all share a common denominator. Obviosity.

First off, you are obviously in charge of your response. Viktor Frankl[194], one of the great fathers of modern psychoanalysis, tells a story of when he was in a Nazi concentration camp, standing stark naked before his interrogators in a dimly lit, concrete room. His tormentors had stripped him of everything: his worldly possessions, his dignity, his health, his well-being, his family, his freedom and lastly, his simple, gold wedding band. In that excruciating moment he had a simple epiphany: "There is one thing they cannot ever take from me, under any circumstance – my response." He chose how to respond. You can choose how to respond. WE can all choose how to respond. For myself, I don't always choose very well. My emotions rise up. My sense of dignity and self-righteousness comes to the fore. And I choose to smack the pie. Bad choice. And not particularly funny at that point. No, it's pitiful. Childish. Petulant. I can go on, but that's pointless. Obviously, I still make bad choices. We all do.

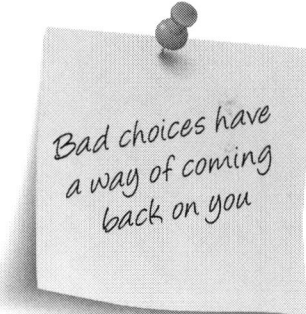

Bad choices have a way of coming back on you

The good choice requires courage and is actually the most healthy. Thankfully, it's the obvious choice, too. My father taught me the "Five Year Test." He told me to look at any particular decision and ask, "What will this decision mean in five years?" It takes your perspective out of the tyranny of the urgent[195], and puts it in a longer term perspective. The decision becomes easier because it becomes clearer. The solution becomes obvious. Isn't that wonderful? Out of the creativity in your everyday life, rises up the obvious choice. You simply have to have the courage to seize upon it and press forward. Carpe obvious[196], dood![197]

The obvious nature of toxicity has long been recognized by people wishing to exploit the weaknesses and failings of their fellow humankind. "Once you've convinced a man that he's smarter than his neighbor, there's no end to the fool you can make of him." Pretty cynical, eh? But quite applicable in fomenting a mob mentality. Creating factionalism. Dividing and conquering. Get the point? The obvious antidote is just that, obvious. The obvious razor you can use in this circumstance is to "follow the money." Now this doesn't have to be physical money, but simply benefit. How does this toxic behavior benefit the one spewing it on the world at large? Is it power? Revenge? Money? Position? Control? Jealousy? ...or any of the Seven Deadly Sins[198]. If you simply follow the obvious benefit trail of the toxic person from their toxic behavior to its source, their motivation will become quite obvious. At that point you can decide if you ascribe to their premise or choose to control your response based on your own set of life paradigms. You can always choose to control your response.

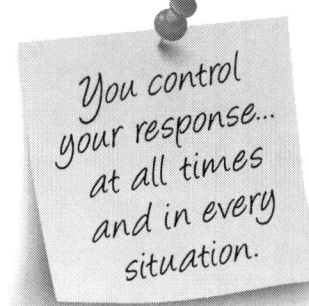

You control your response... at all times and in every situation.

And remember: Toxic is predictable. You know what's going to happen in advance with toxic people. They are so predictable. That works to your advantage. If you know it's coming, you can prepare yourself in advance and choose your response in the cold, harsh, 120Hz fluorescent light of reality – BEFORE the event. You can plan your response. And you can plan your secondary response in case Plan "A" goes out the window. It gives you a distinct advantage over the situation and your toxic tormentor. Predictability is a weakness in your opponent. Your obviosity is a strength.

Toxic situations or people can lead you to believe that you can't escape or manage the situation. Not true. This is where issues like co-dependence[199] or the "Stockholm Syndrome[200]" come into play. Co-dependence is a thorny issue. Not easy to recognize in one's self, even more difficult to break the cycle. Basically, the theory of co-dependence is that one cannot be in the direct, immediate contact with a seriously imbalanced or psychologically ill person for an extended period of time without being affected by the other person's condition. Alcoholism is a good example (among all the other addictive behaviors.) The drinker doesn't perceive they have a problem. The significant other (soon to be co-dependent) sees the problem quite clearly and out of the best of intentions, seeks to shield the drinker from the consequences of their behavior, which only delays the alcoholic from "hitting bottom." They will lie to the drunk's boss that they have the flu, they'll tell the family they're "out of town on business." They'll buy alcohol for them so they "stay home,"

Co-dependence can be broken.

(which is enabling[201].) All of these protective behaviors of the significant other conspire to trap them in a descending spiral of chemical abuse, and enablement. Then, before they know it, the significant other is classically co-dependent and the dance continues until somebody hits bottom and decides to break the cycle. The co-dependent ends up being just as sick as the addict.

The Stockholm Syndrome is very similar but with a bit of a more sinister twist. The victim of the abuse (often the co-dependent other) is physically restrained from leaving, as in the case of spousal abuse. They physically can't leave or sincerely believe they can't leave, even though there is obvious evidence to the contrary. It's a form of conditioning. They end up identifying with their captor as a way of resolving the cognitive dissonance they are currently experiencing.

Back in the bad old days of circuses, elephant "trainers" would get a new baby elephant and tie its leg with a very strong rope, to a very large stake, driven deep into the ground. No matter how hard or how long the baby elephant would struggle to get free, it couldn't break the grasp of the big rope and the giant stake. This training of the baby elephant would continue as the baby grew. Over time, the rope got lighter and the stake got smaller. Until, one day, the full grown elephant could be tied with a little rope to a tent peg and would remain there, even in a tent fire, to their demise. At any point, they could have pulled the stake out of the ground and escaped, but they "knew" it was impossible. It seemed quite tangibly impossible, even though it was quite obviously not.

What paradigms have you tied in place that you know can't be

> *Continually test your "limitations."*

escaped? Really? May I respectfully suggest that you take a step back, exhale, listen to your creative genius, take a deep breath and move on. You'll find the solution is quite obvious. It may be terrifying to you... now. But, the solution is far better than the situation.

There is yet another obstacle you will have to navigate after you pull up your tent peg and leave. That's the wilderness. The wilderness is the distance between yours or others' beliefs about your condition and reality. While you may have legitimately quit (fill-in-the-blank), until perceptions catch up with reality, you will be in the wilderness. Many people quit, or revert, or die in the wilderness before perception and reality coincide. Don't stop until all the cows come home[202]. You've already won the victory. Don't let yourself or anybody else steal it from you because of erroneous perceptions. Grasp the obvious. You have changed. Never let that go.

Consider Ol' Joe. Ol' Joe was the town drunk. Everybody knew "Ol' Joe, the Town Drunk." Well, one day when Ol' Joe was in the gutter and so drunk he had to hang on just to stay there, a realization entered his alcohol addled brain. "I think I have a drinking problem." So Ol' Joe got up and stumbled down to the Local AA[203] Chapter and "took a meeting." Well, Ol' Joe got sober. And stayed sober. He got his one week chit[204]. His one Month token[205]. His one year coin[206]. And people still called him "Ol' Joe, the Town Drunk."

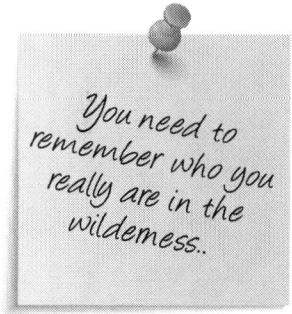

You need to remember who you really are in the wilderness...

toxic

Now since that first meeting, Joe had gotten his act together, got a job, reconciled with his family and everybody he had wronged. He worked the Steps[207]. But after 12 years sober, people still called him "Ol' Joe, the Town Drunk." Joe was still in the wilderness… and only one drink away from fulfilling their expectations. Leaving the wilderness is just as difficult as entering it. It takes trust and belief.

In Joe's case, trust and belief in his "higher power[208]." When he started taking meetings, Joe's higher power was his car, "Because it got him to his meetings and was bigger than he was." As time progressed he began to understand the wisdom of how he was made and began to trust the creative genius in his everyday life. Only Joe knows exactly what his higher power is today. You'll have to ask him. I'm not qualified to answer that question.

Your creative genius will get you through.

Your toxic situation or person in your life may seem insurmountable to you, but it's not. However, overcoming it is more than just a decision away. You must act on that decision. Then persevere until perception matches reality. Trust your creative genius. It's obvious.

In situations where you are not physically restrained, feel free to leave the table if respect is not being served. Disrespect is horribly toxic. In a work environment, it is also very costly… for everyone. We have all worked in toxic environments. I have worked in them, both long and short term. Sometimes the toxicity is in a co-worker, other times a customer. The worst type is when the toxicity starts at the top of the organization and filters down. Especially when it is fostered as acceptable behavior because of the "production" of the offending acolytes[209]. It destroys morale, collaboration and ultimately productivity. It may help an organization meet a short term goal, but as a long term strategy, it is a dismal and destructive failure. Until the perpetrators are held accountable, nothing will change. "The beatings will continue until morale improves." Nothing obvious about that insanity, eh?

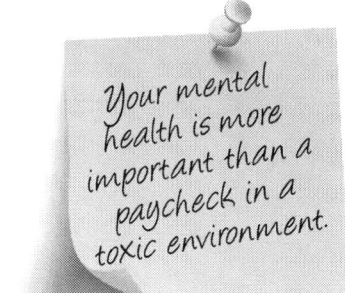

Your mental health is more important than a paycheck in a toxic environment.

If left unchecked, unresolved and unexposed, the environment becomes a pot that is slowly and imperceptible heating up. The co-dependents keep the fire going. The sufferers of the Stockholm Syndrome become the toxic cheerleaders. Duplicity and back-stabbing abounds. (In all my years in the business world, I have yet to meet a booty-kisser[210] that isn't a back stabber. I have yet to find an exception.) The condition continues until all the frogs in the pot are hard-boiled. The rats leave the sinking ship, and the cycle begins anew somewhere else. You don't have to be part of that. Feel free to leave at any time. In fact, the sooner the better.

Thankfully, there is Kryptonite[211] for toxic people and situations. It's called "Obviosity." Obviosity is the quality of being obvious.

Readily apparent. Prominent. Toxicity continues because nobody calls them on it. Perhaps, in your situation, the cost of exposing the toxicity is too great for you to currently bear. Fine. Make plans to get the heck outta' Dodge and work your plan. Perhaps the relationship or situation has far greater value implications than your short term comfort. Great! Then expose the toxicity for all to see. Toxicity is indefensible, unsupportable, unsustainable. It will shrivel up faster that the wicked Witch of the West[212] when encountering di-hydrous monoxide[213]. Toxicity can't stand the light of day. Bring it. Facilitate the toxicity becoming obvious to everyone. It doesn't stand a chance.

Toxicity can't stand the light of obviosity.

Now, in the off-chance that people deny the revelation and cling to the toxicity, RUN! Don't wait. The bigger reason or cause will obviously follow you. There is no place for it in Toxic City. They will still be in the wilderness long after you have transplanted the reason or cause in fertile soil and lavished it with obviosity.

Which brings me to the purpose of toxicity. Despite what you may think or feel, toxicity is not animate or sentient. It's not alive and it can't think. So, what is its purpose? Simply put, its ultimate purpose is to drive you to your creative genius. It's not targeted at you. It is merely a condition that causes you to recoil and withdraw to the safety and protection of the obvious truth. It's a bumper on the cosmic pinball machine of life that flings you back in the direction of where you need to be. Don't fight against it. Just look in the direction it is repelling you. It's just reinforcing that you're in the wrong place at the wrong time. Turn around and see where it's pushing you. It's certainly pushing you away from itself. The "worst thing that ever happened to you" often turns out to be the "best thing that ever happened to you." If we knew from the beginning what all we would have to go through to get where we are today, we probably wouldn't have the courage to embark on the journey. Toxicity actually helps us get where we need to go. The sooner, the better. You just need to see the obvious and act accordingly.

obvious toxic CHECKLIST

- [ ] We all know them. They're obvious.
- [ ] You can deal with them by choice.
- [ ] Don't smack the pie.
- [ ] Toxic is predictable.
- [ ] You can leave at any time.
- [ ] Obviosity kills Toxicity.
- [ ] The purpose of Toxicity is to drive you closer to your creative genius.

notes: _____
_____
_____

toxic

notes: (cont'd...I figured you'd need some more room for this one.)

chap 9

Elephant in the Room

It's already in the room. People are doing ridiculous things trying to act like it's not there. Everybody is uncomfortable. The tension builds with every, seemingly endless moment. Until finally, somebody cracks under the pressure and blurts out…

(*fill-in-the-blank*)

It can be a seemingly innocuous item, an unspoken issue, a taboo subject, a dirty secret, a broken standard of behavior, a person out of place and time, or any other fecal bolus[214] in the punchbowl that you care to imagine. It's obvious to everyone, but no one is willing to acknowledge it. It's the legendary and time-worn "Elephant in the Room."

The cliché is actually quite apropos. Stop for a minute and imagine a 3-ton pachyderm[215] is in the same room with you right now. How would that make you feel? Frankly, I would be more than a little uncomfortable. In fact, I would be looking for the nearest door, or where they would like a new one. How can you possibly ignore it? It's overwhelmingly obvious. And yet, the same people that are in that same room with you now (and that includes you) will act as if it's not there as an ongoing, and daily practice. That's nuts.

Doesn't that sound vaguely similar to the psychological tension that we explored in Chapter 7 – "Cogni… what?" And what happened when that situation wasn't resolved previously? Exploding heads. Tourette's-like explosive utterances. Acting out. Vacation timeshare purchases. (What was I thinking…?) The list goes on and on. There's really no less tension with an elephant in the room than there is in the unresolved decision at the divergence of what you are hearing and what you know to be true. The moral dilemma is real. Very real. And unless you state the obvious, it will simply continue in its soul-sucking state of un-resolution until time ceases to be, or you're dead. The other shoe simply never drops[216].

So, how obvious is that?

Perhaps the biggest cause for an elephant in the room is the Third Rail. For those of you who have never had the unmitigated joy of being crammed, sardine-like with full body contact against people (from whom you would normally flee with all due alacrity,) into a Manhattan subway car in rush hour on a Friday evening, let me explain.

Subway cars run on electricity. Lots of it. In fact, it takes a trillion,

bajillion tera watts to run the entire system. These ain't your usual Joules[217], Verne[218]. And it all runs through a single delivery system; the "Third Rail." The other two rails, upon which the train runs, are the "ground." The power passes from the Third Rail through a pickup that glides along the top of the third rail as the train runs its course. From that pickup, the juice runs through the ginormous electric motors on each car which turn the wheels of the train. As the wheels on the train go 'round and 'round, they are in constant contact with the two rails upon which they ride, which provides the ground link to complete the electric circuit. Et Voilà[219]! You have power and the ability to move/stop the train. Pretty simple.

In most cases, accountability is the Third rail.

But, the Third Rail has a darker side. Unfortunately, it has claimed quite a few lives (New York Subway Super-Rats[220] notwithstanding,) over the many years of its service to New Yorkers. Some involuntary, and sadly some voluntary. Some poor souls who have lost all trust in their creative genius and as a result,

see nothing worth living for in the future, grab the rail. The result is unpleasant beyond polite discourse. Others have unwittingly gotten too close and paid the ultimate price. Hence the phrase, "don't touch the Third Rail." This is often the case with elephants in the room.

To touch on that subject in the presence of those in the room can have serious, if not metaphorically fatal consequences. Let's just say it will change the tone of the room. So, how does one deal with the obvious elephant in the room? Carefully.

First, you must assess the magnitude of the explosive potential of the subject. Is it merely as serious as flatulence[221] in a spacesuit? Is it as powerful as an 800 lb. IED[222] to a convoy of armored Humvees[223]? Or is it a thermonuclear[224] device capable of bringing about TEOTWAWKI (The End Of The World As We Know It)? Your response will be as measured as the compendium[225] of potential damage with which you are presented. Think carefully. This one's usually written in ink.

Lets' start with an easy one; your Aunt Tillie's Holiday Fruitcake. This bad boy has the specific gravity[226] somewhere between lead[227] and oganesson[228]. It will sit in your unsuspecting GI tract[229] and camp out ad nauseum until it finally passes somewhat akin to a kidney stone. Let's

not discuss flavor in this book. It may affect the "G" Rating. So how do you respond at the family table when a big slice is passed to you? Lying comes to mind. "Oh, I'm watching my weight." or "I'm full." or any of a number of "white lies" to help keep Aunt Tillie's self-esteem intact and still dodge that gastronomic[230] projectile. Your relatives around the table will only get upset with you if you "steal their idea." Not much in the way of consequences.

But, let's up the ante a little bit. Let's say you're in the Monday morning sales meeting and the most toxic person in the company is behaving normally, which is to say, without the merest shred of workplace decency or morality and the boss simply lets it pass without comment. Mr. Toxic's behavior directly impacts your work and reputation in the company and everyone there knows it's way out of line. He's the boss' pet. Now waddayuh' gonna' do? The stakes are a little higher aren't they? Everyone in the room is aware of the interpersonal dynamic between you and Mr. Toxic. The boss doesn't care and actually encourages and supports the behavior (ostensibly because Mr. Toxic "performs," even though the facts don't support it.) All the worker bees[231] and the sacred cows[232] in the room are anxiously watching to see how this is going to go down.

Suddenly, everything becomes transcendentally clear to you. A calm comes over your being that is a sure sign to Mr. Toxic of his impending defeat and utter humiliation. You gather yourself, and then speak.

The words coming out of your mouth seem to be coming from someone else. It's like you're watching yourself speak and are truly amazed at what you are saying. You are totally in touch with your creative genius and the event just flows.

Pretty heady, eh? Let's break it down and see what just happened. First of all, you didn't just think of it. The solution had been wandering around your subconscious since you first assigned it the task of resolving the issue with Mr. Toxic without going to prison. In fact, you don't want to lose your job either, because you've developed the comfort-centered habits of sleeping indoors and taking regular meals. Not something you want to place in jeopardy in exchange for being "right" with Mr. T. So dissuade yourself from thinking it is extempore, from your mother wit[233]. It's not. It's well-conceived and thoroughly vetted through the embedded Monte Carlo ("what if?") simulations[234] in your sub-conscious.

In those myriad "what if's" you identified a number of triggers that could begin your calculated response to that scenario. Once all the pieces fall together in any given scenario, you respond according to plan. This is all subconscious. What is conscious is your decision about whether or not a given response is wise. That decision is best made in the cool and conscious light of reason – beforehand. You may think you are responding in the moment, but I assure you, you are not. Unless… you let emotion sway the process, and take a secondary or tertiary[235] response track. This rarely goes well.

At this point, you have abandoned your understanding of wisdom and chosen to act solely on knowledge instead. I think you can see the obvious lack of wisdom in this one. Remember: Wisdom is obvious. In situations like these, one needs to cling to their understanding of wisdom to the exclusion of emotion and willfully and consciously grasp the solution that is best in this particular situation. As you can see, it is all based on your trust in the wisdom revealed to you by your internalized creative genius.

The best tack is to remain totally obvious in your response. Lay out the truth of the toxic behavior of Mr. T. for all to see, in a clear, concise, logical and supported manner (a well-documented "paper trail[236]" comes in very handy here as a way to CYA[237].) The truth is unassailable and can defend itself and stand on its own two feet. If your presentation followed these guidelines, any negative response from the others in the room will be in direct contraindication of the obvious facts as you have so clearly presented.

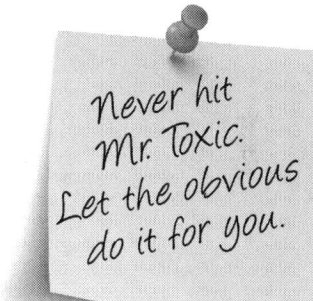

They will have made manifest their own hypocrisy for all to see and have created another elephant in the room. But, this time, it's not your elephant. At this point, if respect is not being served, you are free to leave the table. For there is nothing there for you. Tough call. Significant ramifications. But, you will have obviously addressed the first elephant in the room and made your righteous position manifest for all to see. You will sleep well that night, indoors or out.

But what about the "Nuclear option[238]"? This is drastic and to be avoided at most costs. I say "most" instead of "all" for obvious reasons. This is a situation with often life and death consequences.

elephant

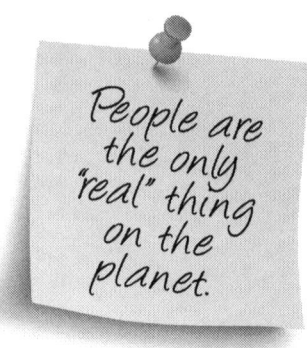

People are the only "real" thing on the planet.

Nothing is more important than life and death because the only things that are "real" in this world are the people in it. This decision must rely solely on total dependence on wisdom. Nothing else will suffice. Touching this third rail will directly affect every person in the room and perhaps many more beyond. This decision is a life changer and must be executed devoid of all emotion. Logic and the understanding of wisdom must prevail. And the total and complete alignment with your creative genius. There is no room for cognitive dissonance here. Hopefully, you never encounter the need for the nuclear option in your lifetime. If you do, hopefully only once. More than that places you in the rarified existence of a survivor victor. If you find yourself in the counsel of that table, you must be totally in touch with your creative genius and follow its still, sweet guidance to the letter. No other tack will sustain you.

The truth is not relative.

The truth is obvious. It is never relative. Relativity is by nature flawed in that it seeks to resolve issues through moral arbitration instead of in the clear and obvious light of singular truth. Without that immovable mooring, the tide can carry you wherever it chooses. It will not carry you where you want to go. Never go with the flow. Only dead fish go with the flow. Swim like your life depends on it, because it does.

So, the question becomes: "Am I the one to reveal the obvious about the elephant in the room?" I guess that's the $64,000 question[239], now isn't it? The answer is in your assessment of the value of any given way to reveal the obvious in any given situation. There is no simple answer. There is no easy answer. If life was easy, anybody could do it. It's not. And neither is your decision. But, the good news is that you have a decision process at your disposal. A process that is tried and true (Didja' git that? I just referenced "truth.") Wisdom/ Understanding/Knowledge. In that order. After you have run the situation and the what if's for all the solutions through that filter, the solution will be obvious to you. It may amaze you. It may surprise you. It may dismay you. But, no matter what, it will be the obvious truth to you. Grasp it. Trust it. Stand fast on it. And experience the greatest adventure of your life. Living the obvious truth.

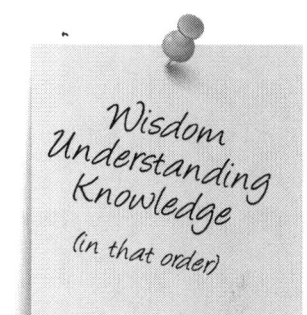

Wisdom
Understanding
Knowledge
(in that order)

So, are you that person? Mentioning these various elephants in the room comes with a price. Each elephant has a different price. Only you can decide if you're willing to pay any particular price. Are you getting good value for risk? Is it a good long-term investment? Is it just a short-term position in the market? Is it part of your legacy? I can't answer these questions. Only you can. But, these are all the questions you must answer before you make the decision to reveal the obvious.

elephant

Be courageous in the truth. Speak the truth obviously as a matter of daily diligence. Live the obvious life. It will serve you well and never betray or abandon you. And even in those times when you think your creative genius has abandoned you, it hasn't. It's still there. Right where you left it. (Didja' get that? "where YOU left it.") Truth never changes. It doesn't go anywhere. It is everywhere. You just need to trust and rely on your creative genius to access it at any time, for any reason in any circumstance. Trust it and act in belief.

Your solutions all come from your own unique creativity.

"So, where's the creativity in all this?"

How you assemble all the disparate parts of the puzzle will be uniquely you. Your perception of the obvious will be creative in that it has come from the creative genius that lives in you. No one can look through the lens that you are given, except you. So, the creativity lies in how with your unique abilities, gifts and skills, you view through your unique lens the situation before you and choose to reveal the obvious and act upon it. It's not about peer-reviewed papers. Peer-reviews only support people who think the same way they do. Creativity is different. Creativity is new. It is fresh. Creativity is what you were made to do. Not conformity. Isn't it time you just embraced the obvious and released your own unique brand of creativity?

Seems pretty obvious to me.

What can be more of an elephant in the room than your unique brand of creativity? Maybe it's only obvious to you. What possible difference does that make? Isn't that the point? It is obvious to you. It is not obvious to the others in the room. Nobody else thought of it. Only you. You put the pieces together in a way that only you could. Of course they can't see it. They don't have your lens, your skills, your abilities, your gifts, your life experiences, your pain, your joy, your defeats or your victories. What you bring out of your very soul is uniquely you and uniquely creative. No one can do it but you. And the beauty of it is, it is so very obvious to you. Why wouldn't you bring that glorious revelation of your soul into the corporeal world? It is yours for that specific moment. There are no coincidences. Only creativity meeting opportunity.

And when that meeting takes place, it will demand courage. So, what is courage? Is it the absence of fear? Not hardly. History is rife with examples of ordinary people doing extraordinary things while being scared silly. In fact, there's a key to defining courage in that exact situation. Forging ahead in spite of and sometimes because of, fear.

I think we can all agree that fear is a bad motivator, especially if it is used in an on-going fashion to "motivate" results. We've all had bosses, professors, coaches, spiritual leaders, politicians and/or "motivational speakers" that use fear as a way to motivate their audiences. Fear only motivates as long as its presence is manifest.

Fear only has the power we give it.

elephant

Once the fear stops, so does the motivation. How we respond to the fear is the significant issue. And our response is always under our control, even in fearful situations. We can let it shove us around and cow our behavior or we can overcome it and press through to extraordinary achievements. In either event, the fear has motivated us and we have chosen how to respond. However, just because we respond in courage doesn't mean it will go well for us (whatever "well" means...) But, the converse of surviving the encounter and living with the relentless knowledge of our cowardice can be a fate worse that the failure that courage may have delivered. Once again, we are in control of our response and can deal effectively with our poor choices, beginning with forgiveness... of ourselves. So, I guess you can see there are always options in relation to our decisions and their consequences. It only comes to a dead end if we let it. In the words of the nonagenarian[240,] Claude Pepper[241], "You only fall off the bicycle when you stop pedaling." That, my friend, is where your unique brand of creativity comes into play.

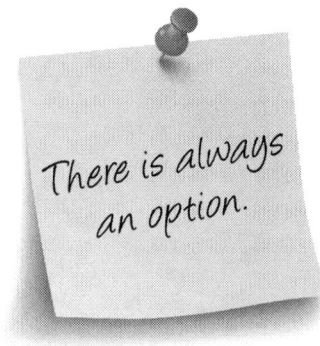

A million other people could be in the exact same position as you are and not see the obvious solution that comes forward from your creative genius.

There is always an option. It is there right in front of you. Only you can see it. But you must have the courage to embrace it. Commit to it. Move forward with it. Irrespective of the magnitude of the benefit you think in the moment that you may derive. That small achievement could change the trajectory of your entire life. Perhaps, just a single degree is all it takes.

When the crew of Apollo 13 was struggling mightily to bring their crippled craft, safely back to good ol' terra firma[242], they were faced with a situation where a very slight divergence in trajectory meant the difference between life and death. If their angle of descent was 1 degree too shallow, they would bounce off the atmosphere and ricochet into space with no way to correct their trajectory[243]. If their angle of attack was 1 degree too steep, they would carve into the atmosphere and burn up in a blaze of disintegrating hope and metal. They had to have the courage to make a creative decision of how to attack their descent, commit to it fully and ride it out to its final conclusion. As you already know, they threaded the needle. Their courage and commitment to their plan of attack is what allowed them to safely return to home and family.

None of us really know what are the "big" decisions and what are the "small" ones in this life. Consequences are beyond our control. Our response to the given situation is ours to render. A decision to bravely speak up about an injustice may create short term difficulties for us. But, what of the long-term? Are people's lives changed… for the better? Or the worse? An Elephant in the Room left to continue in its own destructive path could have huge ramifications for everyone involved. Denial is not the answer.

Small decisions can make a big difference.

Some other tack must be the obvious solution. But, obvious to whom? To you? A courageous person dies once. A coward dies a thousand deaths.

Trust is the key to finding the courage to act in the face of fear. Is what you trust in, worthy of your trust? The creative genius inside you is. Trust it. And then live the courageously obvious life.

obvious elephant CHECKLIST

- [ ] How obvious does it have to be? To whom?
- [ ] Touching the Third Rail is a BIG deal.
- [ ] Truth is obvious. It is NOT relative.
- [ ] Are you the one to reveal the obvious?
- [ ] Creativity requires trust.
- [ ] The obvious requires courage.

notes:

chap 10

The Obvious Lifestyle

"So, what does that look like? Does that mean that I have to lose all nuance in my life?"

Simply put, No. It doesn't mean you have to start wearing loud Hawaiian shirts or trendy t-shirts with a "message." It doesn't mean you have to overshare on social media and you don't have to blurt out your innermost thoughts in a Proustian "train of consciousness[244]." Nor do you have to telegraph your every move or vocalization online like a mind-numbing sitcom or reality show.

No. You simply have to start living in the present. It's all about choosing the red pill or the blue pill[245]. If you take the blue pill, you will necessarily wash it down with the Kool-Aid[246] and everything stays the same. If you choose the red pill, everything changes and the adventure begins. It's more of a decision than anything else.

My first day of junior high was a watershed event for me. Up until that point, I had spent every scholastic moment with the same group of people. I could tell you who peed their pants on the first day of kindergarten, the first person

lifestyle

to pass milk through their nose (in two separate and distinct streams) while laughing at exactly the wrong moment in the lunchroom, or who snuck cigarettes out behind the "colonies" (modular buildings to accommodate expansion and overflow,) and who could be counted on to be hit first in dodgeball. We all knew everything about each other.

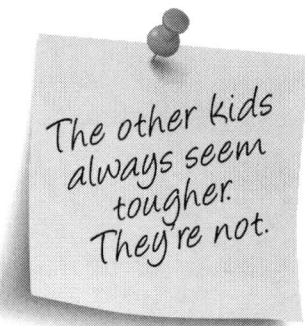
The other kids always seem tougher. They're not.

Now we were going to be merged with two other "feeder" schools, both of which we knew instinctively were much "tougher" schools. Of course, we didn't realize at the time, each of them thought the same thing about the other two schools. Scary time. So there I was, standing in front of my locker ("What the heck is a locker?") trying to figure out my combination lock that would keep all my worldly valuables safe from the marauding hordes. When suddenly, I was shoved, face-first into my locker. Instinctively I spun around to confront my assailant. But no one was there. Then a voice below my line of sight (I was always the tallest kid in my

the obvious path

class...) spoke up in a threatening tone, "My name's Rod Warren (the name has been changed to avoid lawsuit) And don't you ever forget that." Well, obviously I haven't and that was back in the day. "I heard you were talking about me. Meet me after school out by the buses. Be there!" was his nascently pubescent[247] threat.

I was stunned. Here was a guy I'd never seen before in my short life and he was challenging me to a fight after school. And he was about half my size. Go figure. So, I went about my day and left through the front door (the buses were in the back.) I walked home alone and shook my head a lot as I tried to figure out this alpha male ritual[248]. Finally, when I got home, I had made a decision. "That guy was half my size! I coulda' squashed him like a bug! No one is ever going to do that to me again." And they never did. To this very day.

So, does that mean I walk around with a macho chip on my shoulder? Definitely not. It was just an internal decision. No outward manifestation. But it was apparently obvious to everybody else, even people I didn't know. I couldn't figure

out how that happened. It wasn't until years later that I understood. The change had taken place on a subconscious level and somehow my subconscious communicated with others... on the subconscious level. Depending on your life paradigm, it could be manifested on the metaphysical level. I'm not here to decide that for you. You have to go with what's obvious to you, right now – in the present.

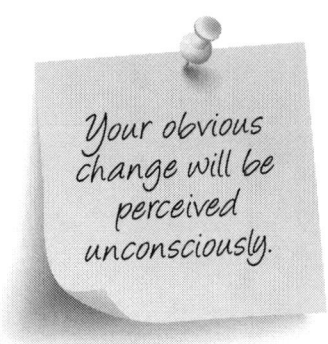

Your obvious change will be perceived unconsciously.

Keep in mind, I don't get into fights. I'm all about de-escalation and if possible, the sneakers option. I have nothing to prove on that level and no reason to do so. Unless, of course, I encounter a bully or a boor. Then all bets are off. Thankfully, very, very few people have ever chosen to cross swords with me on any level. I guess it's just a vibe I have. (P.S. Children and small animals love me, if that's any indication of my character.)

Nope. It's just a decision. I didn't tell anybody about the decision; I just set my mind and moved forward. It's the same process with the obvious lifestyle. When you choose to live it, people will know. They may not be able to articulate what is different about you or even recognize it at first glance. But, it's there. It's like a pheromone. You can't smell it, but it has an effect, nonetheless.

lifestyle

Some people will sense it in you (on you?) and respond negatively. Have you ever met someone and they just didn't like you from the git go – even before you opened your mouth? Or the stranger in the crowd that catches your eye and is just glaring at you? It's weird, but it happens. I've tried reaching out to the people who dislike me before they ever met me – to no avail. I don't get it, but then again, I think I do. They recognize I took the red pill and don't want "my reality" to impinge on their little world. You'd think I had a disease.

I assure you, "obviosity" is not a disease. It's a condition of being. It's not what you are doing. It's what you are being. That's what's so threatening to people transfixed[249] in the status quo[250]. "If nothing changes, I'm safe. Change is dangerous." Too bad. Changing in response to the obvious truth is invigorating and necessary for life itself. I mean, you don't get into your car in the morning, set the wheel, tie it off with a rope and hit the accelerator until you press on the brake and gently slide into your parking spot at work. Ya' gotta' steer the dang thing. And not just in the corners, but to avoid other motorists, pedestrians and unexpected obstacles with which you do not want to interface at speed. The alert and aware ones survive. The ones in the White Zone, don't.

> *You're a human being, not a human doing.*

lifestyle

Don't bother looking for a cure for obviosity. There is none. Once you've got it, there's no turning back. To do so would create far too much cognitive dissonance for any one person to handle. However, groups are another story and another dynamic. There the herd mentality can and will override even the most commonsensical awareness. My favorite example is the lemming. This is a small, furry creature that procreates exponentially. They're not particularly dangerous, except because of their sheer numbers. Some hardwired failsafe switch gets thrown in one of them when their numbers become too great to be sustained by their local environment and it then runs straight off a cliff to its premature demise. This apparently seems like a good idea to its close friends and they too join in the rodential aerobatics with the same effect. Not to be outdone, the balance of the lemmings run off the cliff, leaving only the unaware and infirm behind (So much for that "survival of the fittest thing…") The collective gene pool has been scrubbed and set in order and the procreative cycle begins afresh and anew. Three things will never be satisfied in this lifetime: fire, greed and ignorance.

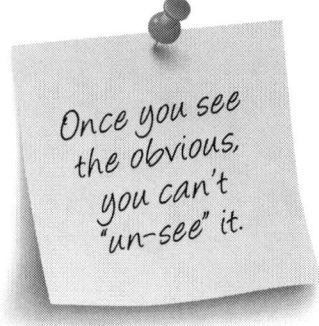

Once you see the obvious, you can't "un-see" it.

I know for a fact that your mother has said to you, "If all your friends jumped off a building, would you?" The answer is,

lifestyle

yes. The peer pressure is just too great. Our desire to "fit in," be part of a group or not be "different" is a powerfully intoxicating motivator. People often in their desire to be rebellious and show how cool they are will become the poster children for conformity. Conformity in thought, word and deed. While the first person who thought gauges[251] and neck tattoos would be a great way to enhance their uniqueness and hireability, the subsequent adopters didn't discover until much later that they were not avant garde[252] at all, but merely conformist followers. Any identifiable group from the beatniks[253], to the hippies[254] to the hipsters[255] all started out as unique but quickly devolved into mindless, banal conformists. Nothing new here. Move along.

True non-conformity must necessarily involve keying on one's own obviosity. It takes courage to "rebel" against one's peers. The risk of being "uncool" is too high a price for a tragically self-snared conformist. Those in power love conformists. All they have to do is groom a thought leader according to the desired outcome and turn them loose on the unsuspecting lemmings. It's human nature. A non-conformist, original thinker is a dangerous animal. They have taken the red pill (irrespective of their position on the political spectrum) and think for themselves. They are in tune with their creative genius and have the courage to act accordingly. That is a person to be reckoned with. An original thinker. Not that their thoughts are original in the truest meaning of the word. Truly original thoughts are as rare as Tesla charging stations in East Cupcake, Nebraska.

All the cool kids think they are non-conformists, when in fact, they are the height of conformity. The variations within the genre are miniscule at best. That's the whole point with clichés. They were original and creative in the beginning. A truly great idea. Then replication set in and they soon became more irrelevant than a hot stock tip in the WSJ[256]. A day late and a dollar short.

"So how do you live the obvious lifestyle?" Simple. You make the decision to be constantly and consistently creative. To do so you must be in direct, regular contact with the creative genius that resides in you. Then you must have the courage to act on the obvious revelations that emerge from your creativity in your everyday life. It's a choice that leads to a way of being. Remember how my decision to "never let that happen to me again" affected my life. I didn't walk around with a chip on my shoulder or tell anybody about my decision. They just knew. I was different… because of my decision. Choosing to live the obvious lifestyle is no different. There is no set, defined methodology to do so. To create one is to defeat the purpose and create a dogma around the behavior that worked for someone… once. It's like trying to create a formula for a viral

lifestyle

video. Not gonna' happen. You can define "cool" and the instant you do, it no longer is. You must live in the moment and steer your car. It's a matter of going. And that's exactly what your creative genius wants to do with you; go. Alongside. Within. Throughout. It is a pervasive infusion into your daily being. As autonomic as your breathing or heartbeat. You can consciously focus on it for a moment and it suddenly becomes uncomfortable and mechanical. Yet, you breathe all day, every day without a single thought about it. Living the obvious lifestyle is the same way. The only difference between living the obvious lifestyle and breathing is that at some point, you decided to be obvious. You began breathing in order to live. Perhaps you have now decided that you need to be obvious in order to live. Really live.

Being constantly and consistently creative seems like a daunting task at the beginning. But, so was riding a bicycle. So many things to think of all at one time and still keep it going in an upright fashion in the direction you want to go. Yikes! But now you just throw your leg over the bike and go. Without so much as a single thought about how to do it. Does a duck think about how to swim? It just goes. It's too busy being a duck to worry about constantly and consistently swimming.

Being obvious may be new to you. This creativity thing may seem foreign and awkward. To those who have embraced it,

There is no "formula" for living the obvious lifestyle.

it is life itself. The highest expression of who they are. There is no reason that can't be you. You have all the equipment. You have access to your creative genius that dwells inside. If anything, the only thing you may lack is a decision. A decision to embrace the creativity that is already in you and live in the glorious freedom and originality that it imbues.

Creativity comes from your subconscious. Your subconscious never gets tired. It connects you to an inexhaustible resource; your creative genius. Connecting to it in a constant and consistent manner is the highest expression of your being. So, why not live obviously all day, every day? Seems pretty obvious to me.

I think the biggest challenge most people encounter when endeavoring to live the obvious lifestyle is getting comfortable in your skin while doing it. It's a major change from how you lived your life before. Your friends will notice it. Your enemies will notice it. You co-workers will notice it. Your boss will notice it. The wise ones will receive the change with joy and celebrate it with you. The others may be jealous or threatened. You're no longer predictable. You're unique, original and totally authentic. There's a lot to be said for authenticity.

Authenticity takes a little getting used to.

lifestyle

I once ran smack-dab into someone's dearly held paradigm by referencing "choice of lifestyle." The use of the word "choice" was all they heard. They never allowed me to finish my premise and only heard a trigger for a pain point in their life. Loudly and emotionally they protested that they had no choice about how they felt and who they were. They were inconsolable and highly offended that I would suggest that how they live their life was actually a choice. And they had all the cool kids to back them up. Then they devolved into classical transference[257] and blamed me for specific events and problems in their life (even though I had only just met them moments before...) The problem was, that's not what I was talking about. I was talking about the choice to live one's life authentically. Nothing more. So many times people hear only what they want to hear and oh so quickly categorize and file their input according to their sacrosanct[258] personal paradigm. They fail to hear the simple truth. Because if they actually heard the simple truth, they may be confronted with a superior paradigm that would actually enhance their life. But, that would involve change. It would involve admitting that what they believed before was wrong. It would involve being real. They would have to be authentic. To them, that is more terrifying than blindly continuing on in a fool's paradise.

> Some people hear only what they want to hear... and then stop listening.

lifestyle

Your comfort zone will kill you. That's a fact. You must, necessarily get out of it if you are to change. To grow. To live. Living the obvious lifestyle means constantly changing. Consistently responding to new and obvious input in a way that moves forward in creativity. No moment is like the last. Why would your response to momentary input consistently be the same? That is tantamount[259] to using the same solution for every problem. Consistent? Yes. Appropriate? No.

Living the obvious lifestyle is about principles. Not formulas. Formulas are rigid. Life is not. But principles can guide you in making the best choices in perfect alignment with your essence in any given situation. Having a healthy respect for the creative genius that dwells within you is a great place to start. Your creative genius will guide you in truth and wisdom. It is inexhaustible. Endeavoring to understand truth and wisdom is a lifelong task. But it bears fruit far greater than wealth and fame. Doing is replaced by being. Once you have developed the habit of seeking understanding of wisdom, you will naturally appropriate those principles into your daily life. Suddenly, the obvious becomes radiantly clear and readily available. You can now wisely choose which specific knowledge to apply and do so

lifestyle

with the full confidence that you have made the right choice. Now you are living the obvious lifestyle.

obvious lifestyle CHECKLIST

- [ ] Obviosity is not a disease.
- [ ] Decisions make themselves known.
- [ ] Cool is conformist. Obvious is authentically creative.
- [ ] Be constantly and consistently creative.
- [ ] Be comfortable in your skin.
- [ ] Living the obvious lifestyle is about principles, not formulas.

notes:

chap 11

"OK, What's the catch?"

"If something seems too good to be true, it probably is." "TNSTAAFL" ('There's no such thing as a free lunch.') Or in the words of the immortal, Col. Tom Parker[260], "OK, If it's free, how much is this gonna' cost me?"

There's always a "catch."

In this case, it's the cost. The good news is that cost is relative. The denomination of the cost may be fixed, but your relation to it is not. For example, when Marlon Brando[261] was living out his life on a Tahitian island that he owned, he would have the Sunday, New York Times delivered to him on the same day. His cost in Tahiti was $10,000. In the Big Apple[262] you could pick up a copy at the nearest newsstand for 50 cents. I had trouble justifying 50 cents for it, but to Brando, $10,000 was a deal. It's all in your perspective.

Project management types like to refer to it as the cost/value ratio[263]. If the assessed cost is less than the estimated value – it's a good deal. If that ratio is reversed, it's not a good deal. But that's where subjectivity rears its less than optimally aesthetically pleasing head. How do you value your

catch

child's first "I love you" picture prominently displayed on the refrigerator? How much is that Babe Ruth Rookie card with the yellow background[264] worth... in bitcoin? How much is your Mom's life worth in relation to the cost of that heart transplant? How 'bout for the convicted criminal on death row? The standards start to get a little fuzzy the closer you get to home.

How important is it to be authentic?

So, what is the value of living the obvious lifestyle – to you? Is it something that might be nice to have? Is it something you simply must have as certainly as your next breath? Your next heartbeat? Or have you simply not settled the matter in your heart of hearts, yet. We have to start with the value to you. "But, I don't know what it's worth!" Well, you have to decide or this whole thing has been just a mildly entertaining exercise in futility. Just another one of those cool things that you might do "someday." It that case, I believe your perception of the value is not the same as mine.

the obvious path

"NO! I simply have to have it… Now! I see how it can dramatically change my life – for the better and the value of it is so far beyond my ability to comprehend it that I simply can't risk not making it my own!" Now, that's a horse of a different color[265]. But, how do you communicate that value to your friends? Family? Peers? The world at large? (without looking like some wacko in a cult.) Not an easy task. One that can leave you stranded in the wilderness until you can clearly and unequivocally define and state its value. How do you quantify an intangible? Well, insurance agents do it every day. All day long. What is the value of an education? Guidance Counselors valuate it all day, every day. What is the value of peace of mind? Spiritual leaders communicate that value every day of their life in terms you can grasp and internalize. It can be done. First, you need to establish your own units of measure.

It's not as hard or arbitrary as it seems. First, you start with what is valuable to you. Then you decide what is the MOST valuable thing to you. How is that quantified? (Don't bail out on me now… We are so-o-o close.) Once you have established

some kind of scale to assess things in relation to what you value the most, you have the power and the ability to valuate any given item or concept in relation to what you hold nearest and dearest. Let's call them, Value Points. Or, perhaps, your initial assessment will be "high," "low" or "somewhere in the middle." That's OK. It's a start. As long as you can evaluate other things on that same scale, you can begin to assess relative value among the various elements of your life. Suddenly, prioritizing your life starts to become obvious. Now you know exactly where to invest your time and devote your energy. Just another of the many benefits of living the obvious lifestyle.

Start with the most important value.

But, there are other ways to assess absolute and relative value in your life. (Yes, I just used "absolute" in relation to values. And yes, there are absolutes in this life as opposed to the relativistic values systems so popular today.) When I use the term "relative value" in this discussion, I mean that it is applicable only to the inter-relationship of the various values within your personal paradigm. It's a closed comparison.

"So, what are these other ways to assess value?"

You are a complex and multi-faceted, carbon-based lifeform[266]. And as such, you have widely divergent perspectives hardwired into your motherboard for use in various scenarios. And they're all relationship based. Relationships with other carbon-based lifeforms. Living beings. The most valuable of which is human life, ranging down to microscopic flora and fauna[267] that enable the rest of the ecosystem to function. These all live and flourish and die in the inanimate world that provides a place for us all to live and move and have our being. There is more. Much more. But, for the purpose of this discussion at hand I will leave it at that. The corporeal world.

Each of your perspectives as defined by your relationship with someone or something around you is different. The values assigned (by you) to them are as varied as the perspectives you have. How do you navigate all those varied value assessments? By using principles. No single formula will suffice. You need principles that are as all-encompassing as the variety of the perspectives you own. It's not that the principle is flexible to the point of being meaningless. No, the principle must encompass the entire compendium of perspectives in your life. The only principle big enough to do that is wisdom.

Only principles are big enough to assess your values.

Wisdom is the key to valuating and prioritizing all the various aspects of your life. It seems obvious to me, that makes wisdom the top priority of things you need to acquire in this life. If that is the only principle that is big enough to fully encompass all the areas of your life, it becomes mission critical for the successful living of your life and fulfilling your life's purpose. Wow! That's pretty heady stuff. (You should write that down or highlight it or something…)

"Is wisdom really the real deal?"

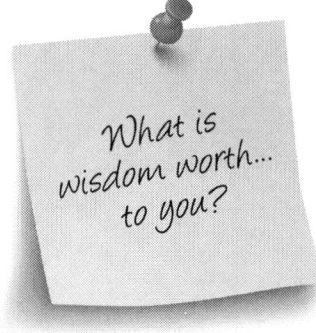

Yes. It's the beginning. The beginning of a journey. You will never fully acquire it. You will never fully comprehend it. You will spend your entire life pursuing it, but only if you're wise enough to grasp that its value is inestimable. It will enable and empower you to valuate and prioritize all the aspects of your life. Then you can establish the relative values of every aspect of your life to each other. As you clearly and obviously establish the value of each aspect of your life, you can assess the cost of attaining it and decide in the clarity of reason, whether or not you are willing to pay the cost.

The funny thing is, at that point, the perceived cost tends to change in relation to your willingness to pay it. Clarity has a way of changing things. Clarity makes things obvious. Obviosity is a paradigm shaker.

Funny thing about paradigms. They shift. They change. They mutate. Once you start shaking up your paradigms and the paradigms of others, stuff happens. It creates a butterfly effect[268]. One change affects another change, and so forth. So it becomes eminently obvious that change does not happen in a vacuum. You can try to compartmentalize your life, but it's just not going to work. Your life is all inter-related. It's all cosmic spaghetti. Everything spills over. Perhaps it's better to think of a change in your paradigm as a change of flow, or a change of trend rather than an isolated and controlled event.

"Change!? YIKES!!!" Yup. Creativity will definitely change your life. Being in touch with your creativity will necessarily mean you will start perceiving and responding (hopefully) to the obvious. Living the obvious life comes with a price. Only you can determine whether or not you are willing to pay that price. Isn't it nice to know that you're in charge of that decision and not somebody else?

Give change a big hug!

The good news is: You have established what's important to you in your life. You have determined the relative value of those things to each other and have associated a quantifiable cost with each one. So, what are you waiting for? Is living the obvious lifestyle worth the price or not? Only you can decide. What's obvious to you?

Let's break it down. Living the obvious lifestyle will necessitate you being constantly and consistently creative. So, what does that mean? First, you must commit to being aware of your surroundings on all levels and in all directions. No, this does not mean you have to walk around with your head on a swivel[269]. But, it does mean that you have to have your awareness on a swivel. Remember when we talked about Color Zones of Awareness? You want to live in Yellow. In Yellow, you are alert and aware of your surroundings, your situation, the tone of your environment, the people and things in your circle of perception and the SWOT[270] (Strengths, Weaknesses, Opportunities and Threats) in your immediate vicinity. No, it doesn't mean you live in a hyper-adrenalinized state of imminent threat. That would burn you out in short order. You're simply present. Aware. You are there in the moment. That's where life is, anyway.

You have to be aware and alert to perceive the obvious.

Once you spend the vast majority of your waking moments in the Yellow Zone, it becomes "normal." Then when you slip into the White Zone, it feels unnatural, uncomfortable. And you head back to Yellow. That's 9/10th's of the game.

Next, you become comfortable trusting your creativity and are conditioned to consider and review it as the next step in your process of realizing the obvious. Once the decks have been cleared of all the noise and clutter, you can clearly assess the obvious and decide your next course of action. To others it may appear spontaneous, but it's really more present than spontaneous. You have already determined your principles and they guide your unconscious creativity. When presented with the clarity of the obvious, your decisions become clear and can be acted upon in a very timely manner. Hence the appearance of spontaneity to others. You're just living in the moment and your creativity makes the solution obvious. Funny things is; it suddenly appears obvious to the others when you articulate its truth. But, they didn't see it. You did. By vocalizing the obvious you have just brought your creativity into the real world. Now, you must choose whether to act on it or not. Once you act on it in accordance to its obvious wisdom, you have brought the process full circle. Whether or not you are able to bring the obvious solution to its full and logical conclusion is not completely under your control. But, the truth of it is unassailable and complete, regardless of its degree of completion. That completion may not be fully realized for generations and/or eons after your demise. The truth will out.

Living constantly and consistently in that obviously creative zone is daunting in concept, but thankfully more mundane and achievable in its execution. Remember how I said, "if I realized I would have to be constantly and consistently creative on demand, all day, every day as a creative director – I wouldn't have the courage to get out of bed!"? Well, it's still true. But, I'm not relying on my own creativity but the creative genius that is inside me. It is inexhaustible. It dwells in my subconscious, never sleeps and never gets tired. People that rely on themselves get burnt out. People that rely on their creative genius, don't. It's not about you. It's about what's obvious.

Now we walk in it. (No, I didn't say "step in it.") Walking in it is a simple and unconscious thing you just do. Robotics has taught us that the human stride is broken up into about eight phases in a single cycle. This doesn't take into account the complimentary movements of the opposing leg or the complimentary and reinforcing movements of the upper body, arms and head. All-in-all, the human gait is a very complex operation during which the brain processes millions of sensory input about changing environment, conditions and conscious control. Yet, we can still reasonably navigate the distance between our bed and the Keurig with reasonable expectation of enjoying a life altering caffeine hit in the morning. Even under less than optimal conditions and Lego[271] landmines in bare feet. We don't think about it. We just do it.

Living obviously is ultimately liberating.

The same is true about walking in your creativity. Once it becomes conscious habit (usually around 6 weeks to make and 2 weeks to break) it will very quickly become automatic. At that point, NOT doing it "feels weird." At first, you'll be convinced "Everyone is seeing the change in me." Nothing could be further from the truth. They are simply oblivious to the obvious. Eventually, they will sense it. You are good to go. Live it.

You need to be comfortable in your skin. This is the new you. This IS you. It is the most authentic version of you that you can be. You are in tune with your creative genius. You are trusting your creativity. You are seeing the obvious and making mention of it. AND... you are responding appropriately to it according to your own previously established value paradigm. That's about as real as it gets. The only "more real" you can get is to take it to the metaphysical level. But, that's for discussion at another time.

You need to count the cost and live your life wisely with understanding and ultimately applied knowledge. Certainly, you wouldn't walk into a high-end, in-home theater business and simply order a custom installation for your home, sign and walk out without looking at the bottom line. Your heart probably couldn't take it unless you're legitimately one of the "money is no object[272]" crowd or insanely in debt. No. You count the cost before you commit. Living the obvious lifestyle is no different.

Commitment turns the cost into an investment.

Not only do you now consider seeking wisdom in your decisions, but you are considering making it a lifestyle. Wisdom is taking emergent priority in your life. Of course you will seek to apply wisdom in this life changing decision. You want to understand it so you can make proper application of the knowledge at your disposal. Living the obvious lifestyle is becoming self-perpetuating[273]. You simply must count the cost. Remember: It's not a destination. It's a journey. The cost will be ongoing.

So, how valuable is it to you to be totally authentic, walking in your creativity, perceiving the obvious truth and manifesting it in your life? Now just compare that to the value scale you established earlier in this chapter and you will have your "cost."

It will cost you everything.

That's the catch.

obvious catch CHECKLIST

- [ ] Most people prefer to live in obvious lies.
- [ ] Being obvious is a paradigm shaker.
- [ ] Yikes! Creativity will change your life.
- [ ] Count the cost.
- [ ] Live life wisely with understanding and knowledge.
- [ ] The cost is the catch, but you have that figured out.

notes:

chap 12

Whatever you do, Be Obvious

Being obvious is not about being the 3 G's: garish[274], gaudy[275] and gauche[276]. It is about a state of being; being in the moment. Aware. Genuine. Authentic. You are very present. It sounds a lot easier than it is.

People tend to spend most of their waking moments either dwelling on the past or on the future, neither of which is where we are. We are in the present, whether we act like it or not. So, why not "be there"? There is nothing we can do to change the past and the future never arrives. We are always in the present. It's very obvious. This is the very crux[277] of being obvious.

Martial artists will talk about this as being "in the moment." All the training and preparation is left to muscle memory and mental conditioning. You simply act in the moment. This is the ultimate ring in the *Gorin No Sho*, "Book of Five Rings[278]." In it, the undisputed, greatest Samurai of all time, Miyamoto Musashi[279] has reduced "strategy" to a life and death game of rock/paper/scissors. Each one of the rings supersedes the previous strategy, culminating in the fifth ring; "The Strategy of No Strategy." This doesn't mean you have no idea what to do. It simply means that you are relying on your instinctual behavior according to the paradigms pre-loaded into your subconscious. The proper strategy will be readily apparent in the moment and your body will respond reflexively according to muscle memory and mental conditioning. No need to think. No pre-conceived strategy will work. You simply rely on your creative genius and live in the moment.

Stay ahead of the curve

To react to the moment is to be behind the curve. You're "right of bang[280]," as Van Horne & Riley[281] put it. "Bang" is the event. "Left of bang" means you are acting in anticipation of bang. "Right of bang" means you are reacting to bang. As a martial artist or a warfighter, you never want to be right of bang. You always want to be left of bang. The element of surprise is a powerful advantage. Life is full of surprises and as such, often has the advantage. But, if you are living in the moment, and living obviously, all the decisions and preparations you made in the cool, harsh light of reason,

the obvious path

be

before the moment, are fully loaded in your subconscious and simply waiting to be realized and acted upon in an instinctual manner. Wowsers![282] That's living obviously!

There is another filter for your actions which is in place whether you want it to be, or not. That is "authenticity." All those decisions you made and preparations for just such a moment are either authentic or disingenuous. Frankly, I don't have the memory to support a lying or disingenuous paradigm. "O, what an intricate web we weave, when first we practice to deceive.[283]" Authenticity is the way to go. The alternative always collapses under the weight of its own convolutions.

Transparency is the lens. If you live your life openly, authentically and obviously for everyone to see, you are transparent. Through you, people can see the truth. That's powerful. You are not the truth, but merely the means through which

Transparency doesn't make you invisible, it makes you obvious.

be

it can be seen. Kinda' humbling, isn't it? I mean we all want to think of ourselves as bringers of value, fountains of wisdom and bulwarks[284] of authenticity, but in all actuality, the best we can hope for is to be a transparent and undistorting lens through which the truth can be seen. Optimally, we have nothing to do with it. Isn't that obvious?

It's not about you.

The thing is, people look at us through that very same lens, just from the other end. If that lens is clear and undistorted, people will see exactly who we are. Warts, pimples, socks with Crocs[285] and all. It's a very vulnerable condition to be in. But, we know from learning about intimacy that we must be vulnerable in order to gain intimacy with others. That process is called love.

Which brings us to a simple and obvious tenet: "If you need something, give it away." Now to the natural mind, that makes absolutely no sense whatsoever. "How if I'm lacking something and I give it away, will I receive more in return? That makes no sense." And the bumblebee doesn't know it "can't fly[286]" and the football doesn't know it "can't be thrown[287]." Weight to power to drag coefficients and aerodynamics don't lie – but they can be punked[288]. (Thankfully…) Giving away what you need is punking the system. It doesn't make sense, but it works. For example, how

be

many times have you heard, "To make a friend, be a friend"? (I see some of you rolling your eyes right now.) Or, "If you want kindness and generosity, be kind and generous." Or the old standby, "What goes around, comes around." Karma[289]? Perhaps. I think it's more in line with entropy[290] and the Laws of Thermodynamics[291]. Some laws you just can't break, no matter how drunk or self-possessed you are. In fact, it's wise to live by those laws, like gravity and the law of impenetrability[292] (which states, "no two objects can occupy the same space at the same time.") Obeying just those two laws alone will greatly enhance your driving experience.

May I suggest you begin applying that counter-intuitive maxim to your life on a regular basis? The rewards are grossly disproportionate to the effort and input. Just remember, it's like an ATM[293]; you deposit some money in this one and take it out from some other ATM – perhaps across town, or out of state. However, it's not a cosmic vending machine where you put in your nickel and the goody drops in your hand. It doesn't work that way. There's often a time lag or currency exchange, but not always. You have to be aware and present to receive it. The return will make itself quite obvious. In its own time and in its own way.

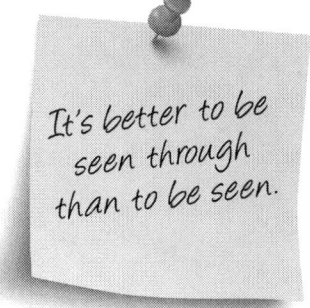

It's better to be seen through than to be seen.

So, what do people see when they look at you through the other end of your lens? Do they see authenticity, duplicity, vulnerability, deception, truth? They will see what's really there, either now or in the future. Obviously, what you see is what you get. Why not let them see what's really you right up front? It saves a lot of time, frustration and disappointment. But, it's scary, huh? There's that integrity, transparency and vulnerability thing, again. Right? OK, so let's start with character.

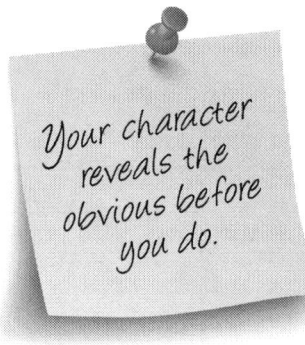

Your character reveals the obvious before you do.

Character is that quality of you as related to social dynamics and commonly acceptable interrelatability. Character can be either "good" or "bad" by that definition. ("Oh darn, there's those pesky values, morals and ethics again. Why can't he just leave them alone?") [*Ed. Note: Don't hold your breath...*] Values are paradigm benchmarks[294]. Morals are the principles by which we aspire to attain those benchmarks and ethics are a personal and/or group subset of morals. Pretty obvious, actually. Using that standard, we can readily assess our own or others' character. (Assess, NOT judge. "Assess" is based on facts. "Judge" is based on values.) Cognitive dissonance generally tends to pop up around this assessment. Of course, our character presents itself through our public and private personal perceptions of the same. Whether our character is consistent both in public and when no one is looking, is called integrity. That integrity can be extended to include our self-image, thereby making integrity a long shot tri-fecta[295]. But don't be discouraged. Developing and maintaining integrity is a lifelong endeavor. Even though it can be broken in an instant, it is always possible to rebuild broken integrity. However, in some cases, it must be done with an entirely new group of people. The distance between the old group and the new group is called the wilderness. See the connection? OWYSIWYG ("Obviously, what you see is what you get.")

When people look through the other end of your lens they see your obvious character and integrity. Is it the one you want them to see or does it need a little "fine tuning"? Let's go over how you can do that.

1. The most annoying person you will ever meet is the person
who reveals the obvious truth. Truth is a whole lot like good ol' sodium chloride. It's in saline solution. It is in every drop of the ocean. It kills vegetation when mixed in with the soil. Yet it is absolutely mission critical for life on this planet. It enables electrical signals to travel from the brain to wherever they need to go. It sparks up Aunt Tillie's meatloaf and preserves dried meat long term. It's trendy from the Himalayas. It makes us thirsty and is on just about every dinner table on the

Revealing the obvious is annoying to the average person.

planet. It gives us traction in the winter (up North...) It was used as pay for Roman soldiers and is even how "soldiers[296]" got their name. Cattle lick blocks of it in the pasture and I like way too much of it on my French fries and popcorn. Salt.

When you speak the obvious truth, it has just as many and varied effects on people and circumstances. It's very stable as far as minerals go, but its impacts are wildly varied. It takes wisdom to reveal the truth in the proper light. Applying salt to a wound would be very painful. But, applying it to a NY Strip[297] done Pittsburg style[298] could transform a great steak into a mind-bogglingly awesome, gustatory tour de force[299]. It's just salt. You need to know how to use it and when. A tomato is a fruit, but wisdom keeps you from putting it in the fruit salad.

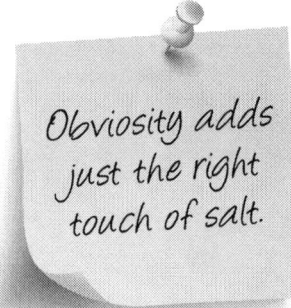

Obviosity adds just the right touch of salt.

Understanding internalizes the wisdom so that it becomes "muscle memory[300]" for your subconscious. That way, when the appropriate moment comes, you can reflexively apply the proper knowledge – simply because it is so obvious to you. Revealing the obvious then becomes more of a moral duty and obligation than a fearful choice. Making wisdom/understanding/knowledge (in that order) part of your being, unleashes the obviosity of your inner creativity. You are at once in touch with your creative genius that lives within your everyday life.

2. Occam had a Razor and it had nothing to do with shaving a little round bald spot on the top of his head. It had everything to do with going against the flow of contemporary thought. At the time he revealed his concept of the direct relationship between simplicity of solution and "best practices[301]," culture and society were ruled by self-possessed, "experts" that utilized opacity and complexity to draw attention to themselves as opposed to the solution. People have accused me of that before, but obviosity always has a way of winning out. My intent to reveal the obvious truth negates my somewhat grandiloquent[302] and circumloquacious[303] bent. (Sorry. Sometimes I just can't restrain myself. I love the English language!) It's not about me. It's about the truth.

Just because obviosity is simple doesn't mean it has to be bland. The art is in presenting the simple with unbounded flavor. I'm sure you've heard the old aphorism[304], "Still water runs deep." The same is true of simplicity. Its long suits[305] are strength and beauty. Not hard to grasp when you understand that wisdom is the manifestation of truth. Truth is simple. Truth is pure.

3. Oblivious to the Obvious is the status quo for most people. So, obviously they will mock you because you give

be

vocalization to the truth that they already knew (but were completely unaware of its relevance to the present.) To compound the matter, they are too insecure in their own creativity to recognize that just because it is obvious to them, it may very well not be obvious to others. The thought is simply too grand to consider. The very creative genius that has revealed it to them is so pure and so simple as to confound their acquisition of it. "It's just too simple. Too easy. It can't have any value." Then for them to reveal this profound truth would invite the very same mockery they dished out to the obvious speaker. The risk is simply too great.

Besides, to proclaim the simple truth would be to admit that the paradigm they lived in before... was wrong. Completely and unequivocally[306]. The transparency and humility would be too great to bear. That's because it requires courage to not only be aware of the obvious, but to speak it – especially in today's day and age. In this world, conformity is king and truth is a lie.

> *People tend to avoid the obvious whenever possible.*

That's why so very few people make the choice to embrace the obvious. The risk to their stable, sheltered, little world is much too high. It is too much for a Hobbit[307] and a direct threat to the Shire[308]. "What would happen to Second-Breakfast[309]?" But there's always one who embraces the creative genius of the obvious... slays the dragon and changes the world.

4. "But, I'm not creative," is merely a cry for help. Despite

furtive objections of artistic ineptitudes, the fact remains: "Everyone is creative." To continue to claim lack of creativity is a hallmark[310] of pride. Art, as espoused[311] by curators and the cognoscenti[312] is as limited as the medium to which it is bound. A sculpture cannot exist as a song. A poem cannot be a pastry. An eternal precept cannot be limited to the confines of humankind's perception. Art is an expression of humankind's innermost being for the purpose of touching another human being. And in so doing, engender[313] an emotion transcendent[314] of message and medium. To limit it to any particular medium is to destroy the message. Creativity dwells within each of us in as many myriad[315] ways as there are human beings. That inner creativity is what defines us in a sense larger than not only ourselves, but the aggregate[316] of all who have passed before us and all of those who are to follow. To say you are without creativity is to make yourself singular among all creation and vaunt[317] yourself to the heights of pride. We are all creative. That's who we are and how we were made. Our life stands as pure declaration of that irrefutable truth. We are alive, so

Pride denies creativity.

obviously we are creative. "Vivo ergo creo igatur.³¹⁸"

That selfsame creativity is from an inexhaustible source. It fills us 24/7/365. It is what makes truth and beauty obvious to you. Live it. Speak it.

5. Trust is the key that opens the unsearchable riches of intimacy and love. Trust is also risky. It involves willfully making ourselves vulnerable to others. It involves taking the first step. Revealing ourselves in a very real sense. This is intimacy.

Trust allows intimacy.

This revelation comes in stages. First is the exchange of totally non-threatening information. "What time is it?" "3:15." Easy. Next, send up a trial balloon and get a feeling for the other person's opinions. Still safe. You haven't really revealed anything personal. Then the rubber starts hitting the road. You express your own personal beliefs and opinions. This can still be done in a measured way by saying you agree with other people's positions. Then the fun begins. You feel safe enough to reveal your own personal experiences and paradigms. This is getting real and is the first authentic glimpse inside the real you. Finally is the indelible³¹⁹ reveal. You share your own needs, desires, dreams and emotions. This cannot be unseen. However, if shared in the proper order, at the right time and to the right person, the experience is enthralling[320]. Far and away greater that all the goofy, silly feelings you have when you fall headlong into infatuation[321]. This is the area reserved for life mates and friends truer than a sibling.

The stages of intimacy are directly analogous to the steps of trust. These same stages must be explored with your own creativity. You must press on until you fully trust your creativity. The good news is that your creative genius will never betray you. Your creativity is worthy of your trust.

6. Excellence out of Imbalance
is a truth many people have taken to the bank. And in so doing, have lost sight of what is important and ultimately lost what is important itself. Excellence comes at a cost. Only you can determine if the cost is higher than the value purchased.

By definition, excellence is imbalanced. Some things must be relegated to an inferior status so that the area of excellence can receive the focus necessary for its ascent to the zenith[322] of recognition. "Something's gotta' give so this one can go to the top." In most cases, everything else has to give way so the area of excellence can rise in quest of fulfilling its potential. This is imbalanced. Once achieved, the level of excellence is unsustainable and ultimately succumbs to a rapid decline, often terrifyingly precipitous[323] and cataclysmic[324].

Pedestals are dangerous places.

Balance is the obvious and superior alternative to specific excellence in the long-term of life. To live fast in pursuit of specific excellence is to burn out and metaphorically die young. Balance is for marathon runners, not sprinters.

7. "Cogni... what?"

Cognitive dissonance is the uneasy feeling a person gets when their behavior doesn't match a closely held, personal belief – or when someone else's actions don't match their words. In either event, the obvious mismatch must be reconciled. A person cannot dwell for any extended period of time in a situation where there are significant, unresolved issues, especially ones that relate to propagated[325] perception vs. tangible[326] reality.

Cognitive dissonance is your friend.

Cognitive dissonance must be reconciled or your head will explode. Fortunately, there are numerous ways to resolve it. But, you must pick one. Denial. Rationalization. Enlightened self-interest. Confrontation. Acceptance. Normalcy bias (Brown Zone). Trust/belief. Choosing the obvious. You can pick any one you want, but you must pick one.

Having trust and faith in your creative genius is mission critical. Without it you will just flounder in irreconciliation.

Fortunately, cognitive dissonance is your friend. It is the early warning system that alerts you to pay attention to the obvious.

8. Obviously Toxic, are the people
and environments we must deal with or be consumed by them. They are corrosive and pervasive[327]. The good news is, they are always obvious and you are in control of your response. You may be tempted to "smack the pie[328]." But, that is rarely a good choice with the notable exception of entertainment value. Remember: Entertainment comes at a cost (Certainly more than your monthly fee to Netflix[329].)

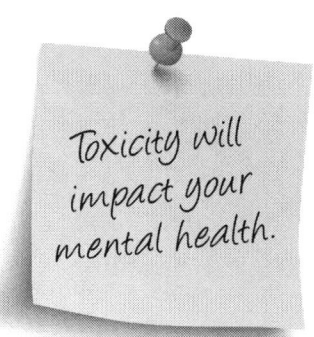

Toxicity will impact your mental health.

Fortunately, toxic is as predictable as it is consistent. Forewarned is forearmed. You can formulate your response decisions in advance. AND... you can choose to leave at any time. Count the cost. Just remember: "Obviosity kills toxicity." And ultimately, the purpose of toxicity is to drive you closer to the creative genius in your everyday life.

9. Elephant in the Room causes
significant emotional and psychological stress. And we all have enough stress in our lives. But, at some point, somebody is

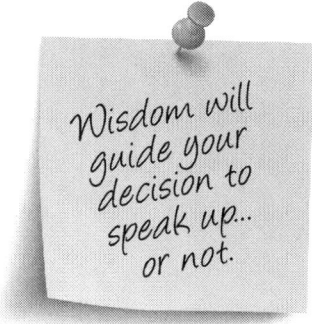

Wisdom will guide your decision to speak up... or not.

going to say something, even if doing so means to "touch the Third Rail[330]." That's a big deal.

As obvious as the elephant in the room is, the truth is even more obvious. Truth IS obvious. It is NOT relative. The question becomes, "Are you the one to reveal the obvious?" Just because you see it doesn't mean you are the chosen one to reveal it. You're going to have to trust wisdom, have faith in your understanding and clearly present the appropriate knowledge… or not. Creativity requires trust, but the obvious requires courage.

10. The Obvious Lifestyle is all about being present. And aware. And connected to your creative genius. It changes everything. Decisions make themselves known in a clear and obvious manner. There is a peace and a calm that surrounds your everyday life. But, you must be exceptionally diligent to protect your obvious lifestyle. Everyone and everything around you conspires to complicate and muddy up your day. The obvious lifestyle is very liberating. As Benjie[331] once said, "The price of liberty is eternal vigilance."

Once you see the obvious, you can never "Un-see" it.

You will stand out because "cool" is conformist and obvious is authentically creative. You can't help it. Being constantly and consistently creative is not "normal." However, it is how we were made. So, be comfortable in your skin. It's who you are. The power of authenticity is irresistible. It's irrepressible[332]. It's obvious.

To encompass your new obvious lifestyle you will need paradigms in place. These paradigms will be founded on wisdom and truth. To do so will require the understanding and internalization of principles, not formulas. Formulas are just not big enough. Wisdom, its understanding and associated knowledge… are.

11. "OK, What's the catch?"
There's always a catch. Revealing the obvious is no different. The catch is the cost.

Most people prefer to live their life in obvious lies. The light of truth is just too harsh. Darkness is much more comfortable. But, comfort has a cost, too. Your comfort zone will kill you. That's why being obvious is such a paradigm shaker. It involves embracing your own individual brand of creativity that lives in your everyday life. It will change everything when you embrace it. So, count the cost. Everybody says they want change, but nobody likes it when it actually comes to their doorstep.

Commitment makes the cost an investment.

The cost is relative to your values. You must determine it yourself. It takes courage to face the obvious and to decide to embrace it. The cost is the catch, but you already have that figured out.

12. Whatever you do, Be Obvious.

Simple words. Seismic[333] impact.

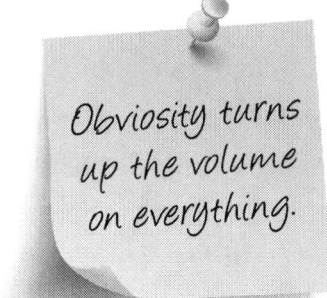

Obviosity turns up the volume on everything.

It's all about living in the moment. To do so, one must have clarified their own personal, life paradigms, established their value, determined the cost they are willing to pay to live by them and then consider the best paths guided by wisdom, its understanding and the application of the appropriate knowledge… at the right time, in the right way. (Whew!) To do so, one must be in close, intimate contact with their creative genius, every day.

Transparency is our objective and the lens through which we can reveal the truth. The very best we can hope for is to allow that transmission with the absolute minimum of distortion. We will never be perfect. But, we can be transparent.

When we are transparent, people will see our character and the truth. What they won't see is if we are true to our character… when no one is watching. That's integrity. When character, integrity and our self image of them are all aligned,

be

we have reached the pinnacle of Mr. Maslowe's Pyramid – self actualization. Getting there will necessarily involve traversing the wilderness until people's perceptions match the reality of where we are. Our goal is simply to press on. Obviously.

We're all broken...

To think that living the obvious lifestyle is something that we all can do in an unbroken flow of self-actualization[334], is naïve. You may start the day really wanting to do so, but before you leave that intention, you will have lapsed. We're human. Each of us has flaws that will preclude us from doing so. Each of us is broken.

Now, I don't mean broken in the malleable[335] and humble context. I mean broken as in a Barbie doll[336] missing an arm and her hair or a Matchbox car[337] that Dad backed over in the driveway with the dualie[338]. I mean broken. But, just in the same way that we can rebuild our integrity, we can continue to get back up on the horse and live obviously. The overall objective is to spend more time in the saddle than on the ground. Ernie[339] puts it quite obviously, "The world breaks everyone, and afterward, many are strong at the broken places."

So, since we're all broken, cut yourself some slack. And everybody else, for that matter. If wholeness is what you lack, give it away. It makes no sense, but it's obvious.

be

obvious be CHECKLIST

- [ ] Living obviously is being very present.
- [ ] Authenticity is the real deal.
- [ ] Transparency is the lens of truth, character and integrity.
- [ ] OWYSIWYG.
- [ ] The most annoying person you will ever meet.
- [ ] Occam had a Razor.
- [ ] Oblivious to the Obvious.
- [ ] "But, I'm not creative."
- [ ] Trust is the Key.
- [ ] Excellence out of Imbalance.
- [ ] "Cogni…what?"
- [ ] Obviously Toxic.
- [ ] Elephant in the Room.
- [ ] The Obvious Lifestyle.
- [ ] "OK, what's the catch?"
- [ ] Whatever you do, be obvious.
- [ ] We're all broken.

notes: _____

chap 13

The Obvious Payoff

Well, this is the chapter that you all have been waiting for. The big finish. The big reveal. The interesting thing is: You already know the payoff. It's obvious.

The good news is that it's actually possible to be on intimate terms with your creative genius, all day, every day. In fact, that's been the plan all along. People have tried to come up with formulas and processes to acquire that intimacy. They have made it more complex than it is. They have perverted it into a way to make money or have control. But, in the final analysis, it's already available to you 24/7/365. Right where you are. Wherever you go. Free of charge.

Your creativity is part and parcel of who you are. You are creative. You were made to be creative. It is why you live. It's why you move. It's why you have your being. It's not something you do. You are not a human doing. You are a human being. And as such, you can claim certain unalienable[340] rights, such as the right to be intimate with your creative genius. No one can stop you. Only you can stop you.

payoff

By being in touch with the creative genius inside, you come into perfect alignment with who you really are. It's obvious. The more transparent you become, the more the truth can be seen through you. (Didja' get that?) The more truth that can be seen through you, the more obvious your life becomes. Things that seem so simple and obvious to you are not simple or obvious to others. That's why you're here. To share the obvious truth in all that you say and all that you do.

Be a perfectly clear and undistorted lens.

Now, am I talking about becoming some kind of wacko, "Obvious Evangelist"? Absolutely not. "A human convinced against their will, remains unconvinced still." People must see its value and decide to adopt it themselves. Anything else is disingenuous and coercive. It totally defeats the purpose. The truth doesn't need a salesman. The truth is obvious.

the obvious path

payoff

A good way to make sure someone is seeing the clear and undistorted truth of the obvious lifestyle is to present the cost. Clearly. Succinctly. And with no sugar-coating. Truth be told, the cost is high. At some point, it will cost you everything. But the good news is that your perception of the cost changes with your understanding of the benefits. What seems expensive now, doesn't seem so exorbitant when you're further along the way. The farther you go, the more you can see. The more you can see brings a perspective to your assessments that is not possible at the beginning. There are no shortcuts.

We are talking about a change in your life that starts with a decision. A decision to change. A revelation of the truth that how you were living before was "less than optimal," and that a better way exists and it attainable. It's not a leap of blind faith. It is about trusting the creativity that is within you and acting like you believe it – wholeheartedly.

Half-measures and sticking your toe into the pool won't work. You have to dive in and swim.

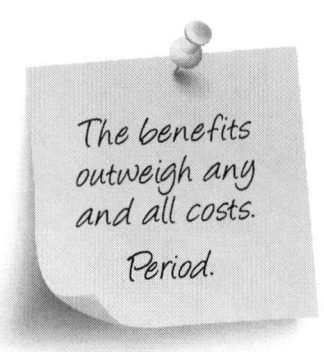

The benefits? Inestimable. I am still discovering them day by day. They pop up when you least expect them in ways you never imagined. But the best part is the peace that comes from knowing that you have an unbreakable bond with your creativity. It will never fail you or leave you. It is part and parcel of who you are. Coming into alignment with it reveals benefits you never could have imagined. Each day brings a fresh sheet of paper and all the crayons in the big box.

As each day passes you see yourself making better decisions, Smarter decisions. Wiser decisions. The stress seems to melt away as you continue your intimacy with your creative genius in your everyday life. There is less uncertainty. Less angst[341]. Less anxiety. Clarity becomes the norm. Miraculous data comes into view as you internalize your understanding of the wisdom you can now so clearly see. How valuable is that? Can you really put a price tag on it? I can't.

I wish I could convince every one of you that living the obvious lifestyle is the very best choice you can possibly make. But, I can't do that. I mustn't do that. You must

payoff

decide that for yourself. Because in the final analysis, you will be held accountable for your decisions, not me. Choose wisely, my friends. Reach out for that wisdom that is so very available to all of you. And once you encounter it, embrace it. Make it part of who you are. Then you will be walking in your creativity in unassailable authenticity. What could be a bigger benefit than that?

You will know in your heart of hearts when you have truly chosen to live the obvious lifestyle. It just flows.

obvious payoff CHECKLIST

- ☐ You CAN get close to your creative genius.
- ☐ Perfect alignment with who you really are.
- ☐ The cost changes with your understanding of the benefits.
- ☐ You get "Smarter".
- ☐ Walking authentically in your creativity.
- ☐ It flows.

notes: _____

_____

_____

_____

chap 14

Closing Thoughts

I guess this is the section for all the people who sit there at the end of the movie and watch the credits "just in case..." Well, no Easter Eggs[342] here. I just wanted to let you know that everything I've encouraged you to grasp and to do in this book, I have already gone through. In my own life. I will not ever ask you to do something I either wouldn't do or haven't already done. That would be disingenuous[343]. I work very hard to not be that way, even though it comes very easily for all us carbon units. We are all inclined in that direction. Some even make their living at it; used car salesmen, politicians, and old ad dogs, like me. But we all have the same opportunity to choose differently, every day, every moment. The choice is simple and within our grasp. It's not easy, but it's obvious.

Being obvious is easy, but then again, it's not. I wrestled heroically with my decision to grasp, internalize and live the obvious life. It just seemed too easy. "Shouldn't I have to 'do' something or give something up?" Well, the answer is, "no." You don't have to "do" anything. You just have to be. You don't "have to give up" something, you "get to give it up." Now before, you accuse me of devolving[344] into semantics[345] and psycho-babble[346], remember this: All the distracters in your life conspire to deprive you of being able to see the obvious. Then, your insecurities claw at you to keep the obvious to yourself. Now, wouldn't you rather give up your distracters and insecurities and clearly reveal the beauty, truth and wisdom that is so obvious to you? It's truly liberating.

Oh, and one more thing (like the realtor says when you're desperately trying to close on a house,) the main point of this entire book was not mentioned specifically or by name at any point. Not there.

The question is:

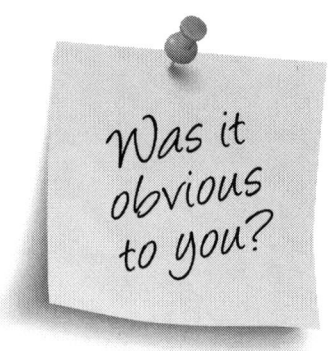

what the heck did he just say... ?

This is the section that will unlock all the myriad of inscrutable[347] references, convoluted[348] allegories[349], "big words," obscure literary allusions[350], contemporaneous[351] cultural memes and esoteric[352] concepts sprinkled liberally throughout this tome of obvious wisdom. Some of the more anal types out there may find this eminently[353] more interesting and stochastically[354] readable than the main text. Some of you may be bored to tears by it. Most of you will find it mildly amusing, punctuated with peaks of vocalized laughter and notes of pungent sarcasm. As my old roommate[355] used to say, "Remember Steve, sarcasm is over the heads of the campers." Words to live by. Conversely, I have the right to remain silent, I just don't have the power...

"A mind is a terrible thing."

1. The "Great American Novel" was a notion that arose in an essay by John William De Forest in 1836. It is generally thought to embody the classical American essence and it is held up as a paragon of American literary excellence. It has yet to be conclusively and unequivocally achieved despite the many self-made claims to the appellation.

2. The IBM punch card was used regularly throughout the 60's as way to interface with customers in the mail. Since it would necessarily need to be returned to the sender in pristine condition in order to be reinserted and read by the card reader, it always carried the admonition, "Do not bend, fold spindle or mutilate this card." To "spindle" was to impale a note on a desktop accessory that resembled a long, thin nail

what...?

set in a cast iron base. To do so, would render the punch card unreadable. Or, with the judicious and exquisitely precise creation of random additional holes with an X-Acto knife (X-Acto is a registered trademark of Elmer's Products, Inc) one can generate all sorts of interesting results ranging from not seeing another bill from the electric company for months to a bill in excess of seven-figures (or so I'm told. I would have no way of knowing about that. Additionally, I had nothing to do with the "Greased Pig Incident" in the lunchroom on Senior Class Day. I just paid my $5 like everybody else to buy the pig.)

3. Post-It is a registered trademark of 3M, Office Supplies Division, without which there would be no Agile Project Management.

4. A serious relationship addiction that affects the person(s) in close contact with another person who is either sick, dysfunctional or addicted in some way.

5. Often considered the quintessential tome on war and strategy. Although generally attributed to the 5th century Chinese military strategist/general; Sun Tsu, some believe it was actually written by a number of authors from 475 to 221 B.C.E. It is in common use today as a guide for everything from combat to business to marketing and advertising.

6. Refers to the amount of calculations that can be handled per second by a computer.

7. That state or quality of being obvious, apparent or perceptible. The gaining of which is why you are reading this book.

8. The exclamation made by the hero of the old tale where a con artist tailor convinced a conceited emperor that only the most intelligent and aesthetically aware people could see the beautiful clothes he had made for the narcissistic emperor. Everyone was too embarrassed to say they couldn't see the emperor's beautiful new raiment, so they

acted as if they did so as not to reveal their own shortcomings. When the emperor went to parade his new finery publicly, an obvious peasant shouted, "The Emperor is not wearing any clothes!"

9. To turn aside from the direct or designated course, to wander. "My mind tends to wander and it's too little to be out on its own…"

10. To rouse from lethargy, to intentionally try to anger or offend someone, to generally make a pain in the butt of yourself for the purpose of getting a reaction.

11. "Positive Mental Attitude", often the mantra of "motivational" speakers positing that if you are always adequately optimistic, everything will work out. Pollyanna had nothing on these guys.

12. This is not an endangered, English wildflower. It is a tersely phrased statement, an adage, a sappy meme.

13. A divide, a point where water either goes one direction or another, like the top of a mountain, or the top of my head if I'm not wearing a hat.

14. A bandolier is a belt that holds bullets and is generally slung over one's shoulder. A bullet in the bandolier would be considered an asset.

15. A fictional character in the 1980 film, "The Empire Strikes Back" by George Lucas. Part of the Star Wars franchise.

16. English author who wrote the Adventures of Sherlock Holmes for the Strand Magazine. He wrote four novels and fifty-six short stories featuring Sherlock and his affable sidekick, Dr. Watson.

17. A fictional private detective known for his exemplary deductive skills. While he is primarily recognized as wearing a deerstalker hat and smoking a calabash pipe, he rarely ever did in any of his stories. The visual was established by

what...?

English Shakespearian actor, Basil Rathbone's portrayal of the character in movies. The image stuck.

18. Although his name is generally spelled "Occam," his given name was William of Ockham. He was "given" to the Greyfriars to be raised. Little if anything is known of his early life. His nickname was Venerabilis Inceptor (Venerable Beginner) due to never finishing his "Masters" of Theology at Oxford. Nonetheless, he went on to become one of the main figures in the history of philosophy along with Thomas Aquinas and John Duns Scott during the High Middle Ages. He died as a political writer under Imperial control. Oh, well... so much for the glamour of being a political hack.

19. The Baroque movement was birthed out of the Council of Trent as a part of the Catholic Counter-Reformation in response to the Protestant Reformation. Its goal was to encourage artists to use ornate art to promote the grandeur and dogma of Roman Catholic Christianity.

20. See: "Baroque" and notch up the intricacy, ornamentation and theatricality (and throw in some pastels.)

21. A state commonly known as "Sleepwalking" where the subject walks around in an apparent state of marginally coherent behavior, (see: "Smartphone Zombies.")

22. Ikea is a registered trademark of Ingka Holding which is owned by the non-profit Stichting Ingka Foundation. The Ikea trademark and concept is owned by yet another private company; InterIkea Systems. And yes, it is not only the world's largest furniture manufacturer... it is also a charity paying the much more favorable tax rate of a charity. Kinda' reminds me of Colin Chapman and FISA. But you'll read more about that later in Chapter 2.

23. "Against the man"

24. Originally created as opposition to Platonism and later it became the main antagonist to Stoicism. This system of

what...?

philosophy was created by the Greek philosopher Epicurus. Its main tenet is shared with Hedonism in that it holds pleasure to be the highest goal of life. Colloquially associated with gustatory pursuits.

25. Eager to consume great quantities of food. (see: Teenagers vs. Refrigerators.)

26. A quadrupedal, ruminant mammal of the genus Bos (hence the common name "Bossie") Think cow, ox or buffalo.

27. French for, "on the contrary." It just sounds fancier if you say it in French.

28. Stubbornly resistant to or defiant of guidance, authority or wisdom. (see: Teenagers vs. Chores, or "Grounded for Life.")

29. A term of endearment used to acknowledge when the character Kwai Chang Caine played by David Carradine in the 70's television show "Kung Fu," grasped a critical concept in his training.

30. Little bits of stuff that used to be part of a larger, single thingie. "The M-80 blew Grandma's geranium to smithereens." (see: "Grounded for Life.")

31. Adherents to the Hellenistic school of philosophy that teaches that the path to happiness is achieved by accepting moments as they happen. It is solidly grounded in "being present." Colloquially it is known as persisting and prevailing in the face of overwhelming obstacles and harsh conditions.

32. Followers of the lifestyle of self-denial. Exemplified by abstinence from sensual pleasures and often for the purpose of pursuing spiritual goals. Often likened to a "Spartan" lifestyle; self-denial and focus on purpose, in this case the pursuit of the ultimate warrior life.

33. A period of rebellion against the Papacy in Rome initiated in Wittenburg, Germany by Martin Luther and continued by

what...?

John Calvin, Huldrych Zwingli among others. It signified the end of the Middle Ages.

34. Zen is the Japanese name for a sect of Mahayana Buddhism which originated in China. It has taken many forms as it has been accepted by various nations and ethnicities. It generally focuses on the emptying of one's self and becoming one with the moment or task at hand.

35. Walt Whitman. An American poet, humanist, journalist and essayist. He was instrumental in transitioning the cultural mindset between realism and transcendentalism while incorporating both in his works. He lived a notably frugal and simple lifestyle.

36. John Greenleaf Whittier. A Quaker poet and abolitionist. A simple New England farmer at heart, yet he moved the world.

37. e e cummings (no, that's not a typo, that's how he signed his work) Edward Estlin Cummings was an American author, essayist, poet, playwright and painter. His simplistic style is often associated with modernist free-form poetry, eschewing the social conceits of grammar, capitalization and punctuation.

38. A formal style of Japanese poetry using a simplistic and rigid style of 17 words in a 5, 7, 5 pattern to express a thought or image.

39. A philosophy for the attainment of happiness through the simplification of all aspects in one's life from the material to the intellectual to the relational. Liberating freedom is achieved through relentless simplicity. Primarily an American art movement that began in post-WW II western art. It morphed into a philosophy of simplistic living similar to the Bauhaus thinking that, "Less is more."

40. A trendy movement whereby the adherents limit their earthly possessions to 100 items. My concern is: What do you do

what...?

with a box of macaroni? Either you just count the box as one item, or leave the movement in utter disgrace.

41. *An architectural and social movement that advocates living very simply in very small homes (<400 s.f.) The movement promotes financial frugality in economically safe and shared community experiences.*

42. *Signifying servitude or submission. From the old Norse language for a slave or serf in Scandinavian lands during the Viking Age.*

43. *A moment of clarity or understanding.*

44. *The Staatliches Bauhaus ("Bauhaus") was a German school of art from 1919 to 1933. Their proposed focus was to unite form and function in art and mass production. Their battle cry was, "Less is More." Much like William of Ockham and Colin Chapman. The primary difference being the focus on aesthetics and the individual artist's vision.*

45. *Lacking the capacity to harm, provoke to strong emotion or offend. Kinda' like the Cream of Wheat (Cream of Wheat is a registered trademark of B&G Foods North America) of interpersonal relationships.*

46. *A structural skin carrying all of the stress and loads of compression and tension with the notable lack of an internal, load-bearing frame. Kinda' like a cockroach, all gushy and schmushy on the inside and hard on the outside.*

47. *A brilliant English engineer, racer, futurist, inventor, original thinker and general irritant to the French. Well worth learning more about. He worked within the system and beat it at its own game. And lastly, my hero.*

48. *DuPont is a registered trademark of the DuPont de Nemours, Inc. A merger of Dow Chemical and E. I. du Pont Nemours and company. Collaborated with German company, IG Farben in the production of the infamous Zyklon B chemical used in Nazi concentration camps to*

what...?

murder millions of Jews during WW II.

49. Polytetrafluoroethylene is a synthetic fluoropolymer of tetrafluoroethylene.

50. A registered trademark of Chemours, a spin-off from DuPont which originally discovered the compound in 1938.

51. A high-performance acetal resin. Slicker than cat poo on a marble floor and much more structurally integral.

52. Another one of those French phrases. This one means, "to call attention to" (like using a participle to end a sentence with), to express satisfaction or approval or suggest an appearance as if by magic. We've all heard magicians use it.

53. Good luck translating this one. YouTube (YouTube is a registered trademark of Google, LLC.) lists it as "fart music," but colloquially it means, technical stuff of little importance or relevance." "Jason went to a trendy, graphic arts college and learned a buncha' techno-poop."

54. This is a favorite saying of CuzBob of the Great Northwet. (Sic) He is surrounded by a culture of a diametrically opposed mindset and this phrase has become a coping mantra for him. CuzBob is entirely too smart for his own good, but he's very entertaining. Who else can you discuss string theory within one sentence then transition to Heisenberg's Uncertainty Principle (which states, "you can't know where you are and where you're going at the same time," much to the dismay of Liberal Arts majors on the last day of class registration,) and then discuss the various gustatory nuances of Cincinnati's famous Skyline Chili, all in the same diatribe. Ya' just gotta' luv CuzBob.

55. Eipper Aircraft, owned by Quicksilver Manufacturing, is an American manufacturer of ultralight and light aircraft. Horsepower to weight to lift are the central focus of their design. Not to mention they are incredibly fun to fly!

what...?

56. *This is the pinnacle of Maslow's Hierarchy of Needs. His hierarchy of needs is a concept in psychology first proposed in his 1943 paper, "A Theory of Human Motivation." It has become foundational in many management and social engineering environments.*

57. *Abraham Harold Maslow was a son of poor Russian-Jewish parents who fled Eastern Europe to secure a better and more prosperous future for their family. He became a professor of psychology at Brandeis University in NYC. Subsequently, he developed his famous Hierarchy of Needs which posits the theory of psychological heath predicated on fulfilling innate human needs in priority, culminating in self-actualization.*

58. *Ryokan (traditional Japanese Inns) are the height of elegant simplicity, beauty and tranquility. The concept of breaking down the barrier between indoor and outdoor spaces is integral to the concept. Matched with exquisite hospitality, these classical institutions are among the highlights of any visit to Japan.*

59. *A traditional Japanese style of flower arrangement. The venerated tradition dates back to the Heian period when they were created for altars. Subsequently, they were used to adorn the tokonoma (alcoves) of traditional Japanese homes. The style is distinctive in its emphasis on simplicity and the replication of totally natural presentations. The arrangements look like they grew in the holders in which they are displayed.*

60. *This is a concept denoting harmonious calm and peaceful unity and conformity in a social group in preference of continuation of the harmonious community over personal interests. Wa is a highly prized condition in a traditional Japanese home and correspondingly rises in importance based on the position of the household in society. It is not to be broken or even disturbed.*

61. *The Museum of Modern Art in Manhattan. Reputedly one of*

what...?

the finest museums in the world. To have one's artwork displayed there is to have arrived on the big-time art scene. Although it tends to be controversial in its showing on occasion, it is an undisputed thought leader and trend-setter in the internationally recognized world of fine art.

62. New York City. The soubriquet was initiated by a sports journalist by the name of John Fitz Gerald around 1920. In his travels to the track he heard stable hands refer to NY as "the big apple" denoting that if your horse was running there, you had made it to the big-time. But it fell out of use only to be revived by Charles Gillett, president of the New York Convention and Visitors Bureau in the early 70's. This time the name stuck.

63. Beyond the perceivable universe. Something "other than". As a form of meditation, Transcendentalism was made popular in the West by the Beatles in the late 60's and early 70's. As related to media, having to do with something other than reality; a digital persona, an avatar.

64. The color zones described here are directly related to the late Col. Jeff Cooper and his "Color Codes of Awareness." They are borrowed here as an homage to his great vision and teaching ability that brought him to the creation of these codes. He was the founder of Gunsite and as a well-respected Marine, worthy of the honor. It is with the deepest respect that we reflect his Color Codes herein to translate that wisdom to the public in general in a less combative form. While his Color Codes are intended for the purpose of survival in armed conflict, the color zones as presented here are for general day-to-day living. In either case, all the credit goes to him.

65. Doesn't mean you're in an ambulance. However, if you wander around before you're totally awake and aware, you may end up in one. It means to have the ability to move under your own power.

66. The benches provided on the sidelines for the players in

what...?

most team sports are generally made of pine. To be sitting there means you're not in the game. If you're riding it, you've been out of the game for a while and very possibly won't get back in it. The only time you ever want to be riding the pine is if you're on the injured reserve list, and even then, you want to get back in the game as quickly as possible.

67. *Baseballs were traditionally covered with horsehide. Of late, that has been replaced by other sources of hide and/or synthetic substitutes. In either case, the covering is very durable and very securely affixed to the ball. To knock the hide off the ball would require super-human batting speed, strength and skill.*

68. *Disruption has become the focus of current marketing trends. In order to break through the extraordinary clutter that overwhelms today's consumer. The thought is to "disrupt" the normal flow of input processing in such a way as to cause the viewer to pause for a moment and actually absorb the message being conveyed. While the concept is valid, the execution rarely is. I can get your attention with the image of a Silverback gorilla in a little, yellow, polka-dot bikini, but will you remember the specific product or service being promoted? If not, the disruption was a failure.*

69. *When confronted with the choice between several options, each with a specific benefit attached, the opportunity cost will be the sum of the other options not taken. Yes, you will need to know this for the project management exam.*

70. *These are the classic choices one has when confronted by a threat. However, there is a third option: Freeze. The common misconception of the process is: "I see the tiger. I am afraid. I run." When in truth the actual process is: "I see the tiger. I run. I am afraid." The reaction is instinctive. There is no time to process fear prior to action. If you do, you will freeze. Often known in business circles as: "Analysis Paralysis." It is always best to establish your planned responses to risks in the calm, cool advance of forethought, not in the heat of the moment. This is called, "Mindset."*

what...?

71. Risk is generally thought of as being bad or shaky. Actually, it can be a very positive thing. When you buy a lottery ticket, you run the very real risk of losing your money and the extraordinarily slight risk of becoming an instant millionaire. There is another side to that risk; you could lose your winning ticket. Vis a vis: The winner of the first Florida lottery found the ticket in a parking lot. That person's only risk was in the choice of bending over to pick it up or not. What was the opportunity cost there?

72. This is a military term referring to a person on "the other side; the enemy." In context, an area of conflict is also known in military jargon as a "theater." And we've all seen bad actors in the theater... Several examples come to mind, but civility and the threat of litigious response preclude me from mentioning them by name here.

73. The Enhance strategy takes steps to improve the capacity, size or response of the risk event. This applied to positive risks by recipients or agents of the benefits and to negative risks by saboteurs. You may work with some from both groups.

74. The Mitigate strategy involves taking steps to minimize the negative outcomes of a negative risk. This often involves making lemonade out of lemons, or if you're an entrepreneur, you make Limoncello with a fancy label and sell it in upscale, boutique liquor stores. This begins to cross over into the Enhance strategy – IF you can grasp the obvious.

75. This soubriquet was applied to Abraham Lincoln in response to his predisposition to tell the truth in an arena that is traditionally know for its lies and deceptions; politics. It is commonly believed his honesty cost him his life.

76. Jimmy became Jim and is the Founder and Executive Chairman of a company called Verisign. They are a global provider of domain name registry services and internet structure. Jim did OK for himself.

what...?

77. Verisign owns the domain suffixes of ".com" and ".net" among others. Obviously, a foundation of the internet.

78. Cardinals in the Roman Catholic Church often wear box-like, red caps called biretta (singular birettum.) Their red brimmed hat is called a galero and their red skullcap is called a zucchetto. Not to be confused with the Linux operating system, either.

79. Crayola is a registered trademark of Binney & Smith Inc. The trademark has weathered several trademark disputes. It's color "Red" has been in existence since the beginning in 1903. "English Vermillion" and "Madder Lake" both inaugurated at the same time, but disappeared in 1935. "Maximum Red" made its debut in 1926 as part of the Munsell Line, but disappeared in 1944. However, "Red" is here to stay.

80. In this case, transcendent refers more directly to the "other than" aspect of the word, as in coming from some place other than me. Something from beyond the corporeal world.

81. The lead characters in the first, primetime cartoon to be broadcast in the U.S. "The Flintstones" went on to be the flagship cartoon of the Hanna-Barbera Productions animation dynasty. First aired by ABC in 1960, it became an instant hit and was the first cartoon to feature celebrities as the voices of the characters. Fred Flintstone and Barney Rubble led us all on weekly adventures through Bedrock.

82. While never officially or even publicly acknowledged, "The Flintstones" was transparently based on "The Honeymooners," starring Jackie Gleason and Art Carney in the roles of Ralph Cramden and Ed Norton.

83. Zip-Loc (Ziplok, Ziplock) is a registered trademark of S. C. Johnson & Son, Inc. It has since withstood numerous challenges of having become a generic term.

84. Velcro is a registered trademark of Velcro IP Holdings, LLC.

what...?

Swiss Engineer, Georges de Mestral went for a walk with his dog in 1941 and came back with a bunch of burrs on himself and his dog. After closer examination, the idea of hook and loop became very obvious to him. He combined "velvet" and "crochet" to create the now ubiquitous name of his new invention – Velcro. Nylon was a new invention and he put it to good use in the manufacture of Velcro. For decades he struggled to keep the name "Velcro" from becoming generic, and has been successful. Not all hook and loop is Velcro, but all Velcro is hook and loop.

85. Keurig is a registered trademark of Keurig Inc. They are responsible for millions of people becoming ambulatory and sentient every morning around the world. The designs may vary, but the miracle of the articulated joint on the top section of the device is not lost on this author. May it ever fascinate me as I watch and patiently wait as it dispenses sanity to me every morning. Long live Keurig.

86. The safety pin was invented by Walter Hunt as he idly fiddled with a piece of wire trying to figure out how to repay a $15 debt. He patented the safety pin in 1849 and sold the patent to his creditor for $400. Obviously, a good return on his investment.

87. While the Flow-Bee was invented by Rick E. Hunts in 1986, its primary competitor, the RoboCut was patented two years earlier. Both utilize a vacuum system that suctions up the hair while an electric razor trims it to a specified and uniform length. FlowBee had much more media presence in those endearing, late-night TV commercials of happy people getting perfect haircuts by Mom, Dad or by themselves. A Shop-Vac (registered trademark of Shop-Vac USA, Inc.) and an electric hedge clippers is far more entertaining and has the added element of dangerous excitement. Flow-Bee won the roll-out.

88. The Post-It product (a registered trademark of the 3M Company) is based on a "failed" super-strength adhesive invented by Spencer Silver in 1968. Although Silver

didn't immediately "see" the obvious application for this unique, re-usable product, Art Fry did. Originally released by 3M as "Press 'n Peel," the product didn't immediately take-off. But once it did, "It spread like a virus!!" said Fry. Now they're everywhere and we're stuck with them... literally, albeit removably.

89. Charles Goodyear, the name eponymous with his company famous for tires, accidentally stumbled upon "Vulcanization" as a way of hardening and strengthening rubber.

90. Goodyear discovered that while heating accomplished some benefit in hardening and strengthening natural rubber, it was only when he accidentally dumped sulfur in with his natural rubber in a hot frying pan that he saw a significant improvement. In amazement, he watched as the rubber got harder and stronger as time went on. He patented the accident five years later in 1844. Subsequently, zinc oxide was used in tire making to add durability and strength. But, due to the need for zinc oxide in battlefield medicine during World War I, a substitute was necessary to meet both the need for tires and medicine. Carbon black became the preferred substitute and was collected by scraping the ceilings of galvanized steel rooms filled with massive amounts of smoldering wicks from kerosene lamps. That's why tires are black today, instead of the original white color imparted by the zinc oxide to the rubber.

91. It just sounds so much cooler when you say it in French. I could have just said, "reason for existence," but where's the fun in that?

92. In the 14th century in Europe, armorers began to make an articulated, metal-plated glove to protect a combatant's hands during battle. To challenge an opponent, a knight would throw down (another challenge term) one of his gauntlets at the feet of the person being challenged. If the other person picked up the gauntlet (yet another challenge term) it meant the challenge was accepted. The person bending down to pick up the gauntlet was momentarily at a

what...?

significant disadvantage to the challenger. Occasionally, the knights were chivalrous and allowed for the challenged to stand up before beginning the personal combat.

93. A term bandied about by financial types (I can say that because I was one. You know, Series 7, financial planner and all that.) to communicate that they would be behaving in the best interests of the client.

94. An open flamed burner using any of a variety of gas types to heat, sterilize and/or combust in a laboratory environment. This nifty little gizmo was invented by Robert Bunsen in 1855 (from a design by Peter Desega, who more than likely modified an earlier design by Michael Faraday, Father of Electromagnetic Field Theory, and creator of the "Faraday Cage" long before the invention of EMP's.) Little did Faraday dream that in the future you could protect critical electronics, supported by crinkled cellophane in a disused microwave oven in the event of one of those nasty ol' EMP's. But I digress...

95. More commonly known as "The Great Ice Age." It occurred between 2.6 million and 11,700 years ago according to the International Union of Geological Sciences. So, who's gonna' challenge them? Nobody alive now was alive then. And they gave themselves just shy of 2.6 million years of wiggle room.

96. Today it is listed as a CoC (Chemical of Concern) and its production has been discontinued. Its chemical composition was naptha, petroleum and light atiphatic. It has been soundly condemned at numerous Earth Day events along with the insidious dihydrous monoxide which is used by corporations, found in pesticides and known to cause death in humans according to Penn and Teller.

97. There's that French again. Doncha' jus' luv it? No, it doesn't mean a "piece of resistance." It means, "the most important feature," or "an outstanding accomplishment." Just say it with conviction using a heavy French accent.

what...?

98. Zippo is a registered trademark of the Zippo Manufacturing company. This is the classic and quintessential lighter used extensively throughout the world and clicked to life in 1932. In fact, they even trademarked the signature "click" that the lighter makes when it is opened. My most memorable product placement of a Zippo was at the end of the 2008 movie "Gran Torino" when Clint Eastwood reached for his... one last time.

99. Also known as contrabass. It is the lowest vocal range for a singer and ranges from four notes above middle C to the second E below middle C. The operatic bassi profundi (plural) can resonate from their toenails, much like Lou Rawls in the morning or Barry White with a cold.

100. With a first name like "Marion," the iconic John Wayne had to grow up tough (and change his name once he got to Hollywood.)

101. There's that pesky French, again. Sheesh! They got a different word for everything! This time it means, "an accomplished thing," probably irreversible. Kinda' like writing that snarky nastygram about the CEO's totally inane "All Hands" conference call, in response to the company wide "Recap" email while venting to your buddy, and then hitting "Reply All."

102. Cleaning up massive corporate, toxic messes since 1980. This program "is responsible for cleaning up some of the nation's most contaminated land and responding to environmental emergencies, oil spills and natural disasters. To protect public health and the environment, the Superfund program focuses on making a visible and lasting difference in communities, ensuring that people can live and work in healthy, vibrant places." According to the EPA website.

103. Environmental Protection Agency.

104. Latin sounds kinda' cool, too. This means, "to infinity." On and on, endlessly, forever. Kinda' like 10th grade Algebra II.

what...?

105. Latin again. This time it means, "to the point of nausea." e.g.: Riding the virtual rollercoaster 17 times in a row after wolfing down two chili dogs, an entire cotton candy, a deep-fried pickle, two funnel cakes and a super-size butter beer at the theme park. It ain't purty (but it is colorful. - see: "Technicolor Yawn.").

106. The Japanese are traditionally very modest, the women especially. The act of opening one's kimono is reserved exclusively for the viewing of one's husband and as such is a very personal reveal. One that requires complete trust.

107. Baccarat Crystal is a registered trademark of Baccarat since 1860, in Paris, France. It represents the pinnacle of fine crystal made in France and is world-renowned as a highly sought after luxury item.

108. These odorless, tasteless and invisible secreted or excreted chemical factors wreak havoc in Middle Schools. Not only are the kids' hormones doing jumping jacks, the air is thick (figuratively) with exuberant pheromones who's only purpose is to trigger a social response among members of the same species. My favorite response to these invisible motivators is on "Star Trek – The Next Generation" when the Enterprise was tasked with transporting a royal concubine who was a species known for their incredible concentration of uber-powerful pheromones. When she was brought on the bridge for introductions, Worf howled. 'Nuff said.

109. "Why couldn't he just say, 'Don't judge a book by its cover.'" [Ed. Note: Where's the fun in that?]

110. Albert Einstein was known for not only being absent-minded, but for his inability to drive. Subsequently, he needed a chauffeur to get around to his various speaking engagements. In that day and age, his picture was not widely circulated, so very, very few people actually knew what he looked like. One evening on the way to yet another speaking engagement about his new-fangled Theory of Relativity, he commented to his driver that he was just too

what...?

tired to give the same speech again that night. But, the show must go on. So, the driver, who had sat in on all of his carbon copy lectures offered to give the speech for him since no one knew what he looked like and the audiences always asked the same questions afterward. Einstein agreed and donned the chauffeur's cap while they were out of sight at the venue and followed his driver inside, and sat in the back of the room. The speech went off without a hitch. During the Q&A, one of the audience came up with a question that the driver simply didn't know. Without so much as a pause or blink of the eye, the driver said, "Please forgive me, but that question is so basic, I will have my chauffeur answer it for you." Obviously a smart driver.

111. Ever wonder why you can't ever seem to make a dent in your mortgage or make any headway on paying off your credit card? Besides being planned that way, here's why. The miracle of Compound Interest. (Not a miracle for you – for the banks...) The rule is simply a compound interest calculator. It will tell you how long and at what interest rate it will take for an investment to double in size. e.g.: The years to double equals 72 divided by the interest rate. Simple. You can substitute either of the variables with known values to find the third value. The answer will always surprise you, and rarely pleasantly. (Unless of course, you bought Microsoft stock back in 1974. But then again, you wouldn't be reading this book. You'd be writing your own.)

112. MasterCard is a registered trademark of MasterCard, Inc. It started life as Master Charge back in 1966 as part of the Interbank Card Association and became MasterCard in 1979.

113. Leroy Jethro Gibbs is a fictional character in the CBS show "NCIS." He is reputed to have had 4 wives in the story. Mark Harmon, who plays the part of Gibbs, has only had one wife; Pam Dawber of "Mork and Mindy" fame.

114. An exceptionally bad tactic for any fighter. It means to arrogantly thrust your chin forward to make it easily

what...?

accessible to a debilitating blow by one's opponent. Unless you know how your opponent will respond and have your own response planned, ready and are able to deploy it effectively, it will not go well for you.

115. Incapable of recognizing or caring about the feelings of others or comprehending how their behavior will affect them. A psychological disorder characterized by anti-social behavior. We've all met these people before.

116. An archaic group of humans known as Homo Sapiens Neanderthalensis. Thought to be extinct at least 24,000 years ago, recent sightings in the cheap seats at pro football games have discredited this carbon dating-based notion.

117. This is the world we can perceive. Also known as an "Uncategorized Spell" in World of Warcraft, at least as of patch 9.1.0. If you know what I just said, you need to get out more often...

118. Macbeth is the lead character in "The Scottish Play" (Macbeth). Superstition has it that one should never mention the name "Macbeth" around the theater because it will bring bad luck. Hence the soubriquet. The speech comes from Act 5: Scene 5.

119. Known as the god of dreams, son of Somnus. The name derives from Ancient Greek meaning, "form, shape." He is known to form and shape human dreams and purportedly appears in human form in them.

120. To chew one's cud. Generally associated with an animal with multiple stomachs (or partitions) to accommodate the digestion of vegetable matter. The animal regurgitates the contents of the first "stomach" to rechew it. Ewwwwwww... Gross!

121. This is a cool kid marketing catch phrase. It means to attain first position in top page ranking in the targeted audience's personal recall. Sounds really good in marketing presentations.

what...?

122. After you dance to the tune, you must pay the musician for services rendered.

123. Mona Burrows-Andrews is the woman responsible for the inception of this book you hold in your hands. I serendipitously met her on a flight to Texas and over the course of the next few hours, this total stranger became a friend and insisted I write a book. Well, here it is. Thanks Mona, for shoving me in the pool. Mona is a successful Speakers Agent/Coach and Certified Professional Life Coach as well as an exceptionally smart and intuitive woman.

124. A French term used to designate a climb in a bicycle stage race (most notably the Tour de France) that is above and beyond the most difficult categorized climb in the race – Category 1. It means, "beyond categorization." Suffice it to say, it doesn't get any tougher than this...

125. Terms of endearment for my fellow community residents out here at the shallow end of the limited gene pool where I live.

126. Another quote from my old roommate when I was single. Richard ran the legendary Steinmetz Home for Wayward Boys.

127. Standard announcement of conquest by the Borg of "Star Trek – The Next Generation" fame. I always wondered what would happen if the Borg met the Death Star of "Star Wars" fame. "What happens when an immovable object meets an irresistible force?" (They become one...) Now all the physics majors are writhing in their seats, not to mention the hordes of Trekkers and Star Warriors.

128. The purpose of the game is to show how quickly and egregiously communication breaks down in transmission. In a group of people, a message is whispered in the ear of the first player. They then whisper the message to the next player and so forth until the message has passed through the entire group. Inevitably, the message is distorted beyond

what...?

recognition when it comes out the other end of the chain.

129. A somewhat cynical phrase, often attributed to Winston Churchill, but its true origins are unknown. Obviously, all historical accounts are true, otherwise why would Abraham Lincoln have said, "Everything on the internet is true."

130. Alexis Charles Henri Clerel, comte de Tocqueville came from aristocratic roots, but became remarkably insightful into human behavior because of his political philosophy and diplomatic skills.

131. Charles Stewart Rolls was a Welsh pioneer in motoring and aviation. He joined up with a crane manufacturer to build "The best Car in the world." He was the first Briton to die in an aeronautical accident while flying a Wright Brothers plane.

132. Sir Henry Frederick Royce, 1st Baronet was an English crane engineer known for his car designs and airplane engines that enjoyed a well-deserved reputation for longevity and reliability. He partnered with Charles Rolls and Claude Johnson in 1904 in starting the motorcar company that still bears his name.

133. The last queen of France before the French Revolution during which she lost her head after the famous quote of "Let them eat cake!" when asked what should the starving peasants eat.

134. Scratch.

135. Belch.

136. Fart.

137. Jonathan ("Jonny") Kim is the quintessential poster child for overachievement. This is what a real American Hero looks like.

138. Sea, Air and Land – The United States Navy SEALs are

what...?

the primary special operations force and a component of the Naval Special Warfare Command. These are the best of the best.

139. Basic Underwater Demolition School - BUD/S Orientation is a three-week course that introduces candidates to Coronado, the Naval Special Warfare Center and the BUD/S lifestyle. During Orientation, Navy SEAL instructors introduce candidates to BUD/S physical training, the obstacle course and other unique training aspects. Many of these skills have their roots in the Frogman tradition of the Vietnam era.

140. "The Adventures of Ozzie and Harriet" was a popular TV show which debuted in 1952. It was the longest running comedy series in America until it was surpassed by "The Simpsons" in 2004. Continuity freaks will remember the casual, throwaway sight gag that Ozzie did in the latter years' show opener, where he is pictured on the edge of the obligatory twin bed and rocks back while simultaneously pulling on both legs of his pants at the same time and then seamlessly standing up to button his pants and buckle his belt. Yup, Ozzie wasn't like everybody else.

141. Trekkies will remember that this is a quote from Dr. Leonard "Bones" McCoy played by DeForest Kelley in the original "Star Trek" series. It was generally preceded by a frustrated, "Dammit, Jim! I'm just a..."

142. Overly rapid heartbeat. Think, walking around a corner and unexpectedly bumping into your crush.

143. An anti-human thymocyte immunoglobulin preparation made of purified polyclonal antibodies derived from rabbits. In the words of the iconic Mel Blanc, "Ehhhh... What's up, Doc?"

144. I made this one up. I just needed something that sounded really medical/technical. In retrospect, perhaps I should have added some Latin, or called a neurologist friend of mine.

what...?

145. *"Beating a dead horse." It has about the same efficacy as threatening to ground a teenager for not cleaning their room...*

146. *A paradoxical or insoluble riddle in which a fanciful question is answered by a pun. A pun is very much like flatulence in that the author enjoys them the most.*

147. *Not to be confused with High Altitude Low Opening. That highly trained paratrooper skill will not help you when you get "booted upstairs." (Unless you have a "Golden Parachute" – a well thought out and well-funded exit strategy.)*

148. *Dr. Lawrence J. Peter developed "The Peter Principle" of management which explains why there is an inordinate amount of incompetency the higher one rises in an organization.*

149. *Having the same name as the founder/author.*

150. *Said by the fictitious character Lucy Ricardo played by Lucille Ball in the eponymously titled TV show, "I Love Lucy" in the 50's. When catching her husband Ricky Ricardo (played by her real-life husband, Desi Arnaz) in some comic misbehavior, she would mock his Cuban accent while holding his feet to the fire.*

151. *A project management or financial investment assessment whereby a client's willingness to tolerate risk (positive or negative) is quantified for the purpose of planning.*

152. *A person who only does one thing well.*

153. *Oscar Fingal O'Flahertie Wills Wilde was a celebrated playwright and poet during the 1880's. He is best known for his novel "The Picture of Dorian Gray" and his comedic play, "The Importance of Being Earnest." He was the subject of what could arguably be the first celebrity trial for homosexuality. He died of meningitis at the age of 46.*

what...?

154. Best known by his nom de plume, Mark Twain. ("There's that pesky French again. When is he ever going to give that stuff up?!") [Ed. Note.: Probably never.]

155. General George Smith Patton, Jr. was known disparagingly by his men for his apparent total disregard of the danger to or welfare of the men under his command. He is reputed as only being interested in winning... at any cost.

156. Since I don't believe in coincidence, let's just call this, "chance."

157. This is a really cool word I added to my collection back in the early 70's when I first saw it on the sign of a head shop near the campus in Cincinnati. It means, "finding really cool stuff you hadn't been looking for."

158. A 20th century social psychologist who countered the dominant behaviorist view of social psychology which posited that stimulus-response conditioning was the primary driver for human behavior. His theories of cognitive dissonance and social comparison pointed out the obvious inadequacies of this generally accepted theory.

159. Depending on condition, this model ranges from $54,999.99 to obviously stupid money in today's market.

160. Available for well under $80 depending on model and features chosen.

161. Headline for a General Mills "Total" Cereal ad in 1965 stereotypically showing a mother fretting about her teenage daughter's penchant for diets and how to get the proper nutrition in her. By today's standards, this vintage ad would not be published for obvious reasons...

162. William Griffith Wilson, also known as "Bill W." and Robert Holbrook Smith ("Dr. Bob") co-founded Alcoholics Anonymous. They developed the "Twelve Steps" as a foundational structure for alcoholics to gain and retain sobriety. Members of A.A. often refer to themselves as

what...?

"friends of Bill W."

163. The size of the "Big Box" of Crayolas has changed over the years, but the original had 64 colors and a sharpener built into the back of the box. Currently the Big Box comes in 96 and 120 versions.

164. Merriam-Webster is a registered trademark of Merriam-Webster, Inc. The company began in the 18th century in America with the venerable Noah Webster. In 1843, after Noah's death, George Merriam George and Charles Merriam founded the company as G & C Merriam Co, and purchased the rights to Webster's Dictionary.

165. Theodore Robert Cowell, later Bundy, was a prolific serial killer during the 70's and confessed to the abduction, rape and murder of 30 young women and girls.

166. He was an American serial killer who assaulted and murdered at least 33 young men and boys.

167. Yet another financial term used to define the rationalization for giving money to one's charity of choice in lieu of paying the same amount in taxes.

168. Gilles de la Tourette identified a neurodevelopmental disorder characterized by multiple motor tics such as blinking, coughing, throat clearing, sniffing and facial movements. These tics are accompanied by at least one vocal tic, including sudden, loud and uncontrollable outbursts and use of foul language that would not normally be used by the person exhibiting the behavior. The effect tends to be startling to bystanders.

169. Anyone who has ever closed a bar has heard this one.

170. My neighbor Mark, was born missing some fingers on both hands and a club foot. He learned to cope early on and has not let it hold him back on any level, except perhaps "piano playing." He delights in diffusing situations by drawing humorous attention to his missing digits. "I'd give you a

what...?

hand, but I'm fresh out." To know him is to love him.

171. A cognitive bias that leads people to disbelieve or minimize imminent danger. It is a coping mechanism for stress that is based on denial. "Everything's going to be OK. I'm just looking forward to getting back to normal." Self-deception is the worst kind.

172. Genus designation for "ducks." (And you were expecting...?)

173. Shouted at the fictitious character "Forrest Gump" in the movie by the same name played by Tom Hanks. And Forrest just kept running... till he was done.

174. The fictitious character was created by Scottish novelist and playwright J. M. Barrie and later converted into a theatrical version that has thrilled and delighted children for generations. Peter Pan Syndrome is defined as the psychological disorder where the subject steadfastly and stoutly refuses to grow up. "You're only young once, but you can be immature forever."

175. A fictitious fairy character in the play version of the story. She drinks poison intended for Peter Pan and begins to die. Peter calls on the audience of children to clap their hands if they believe that Tinker Bell will survive. He builds the intensity of the moment until "Tink" recovers because of the "faith" of the audience.

176. When 45's (vinyl records played at 45 RPM) were all the rage, they were used to promote individual songs known as "singles." Since the records had two sides, the record companies didn't want to waste the second side, so they put another song by the same artist on the other side. Since you had to flip the record over to play the other side, it became known as the "flipside." Ironically, the flipside of 45's often became the "hit" and the "A" side fell into obscurity.

177. Decimus Junius Juvenalis was a Roman poet in the late 1st and early 2nd century C.E. He is best known for his

what...?

collection of satirical poems known as "The Satires." He is commonly remembered for his pithy quotes, "Who will watch the watchers?"; "Never does Nature say one thing and Wisdom another."; "Many commit the same crime with a very different result. One bears a cross for his crime and another a crown."

178. When referring to Caesar's method for placating the populace he lamented that the Roman populace readily relinquished its civic duties for the free grain and games in the Circus Maximus in Rome by those seeking or currently in power. The full quote is, "The people who formerly gave military power, high offices, legions, all, now contains itself, and eagerly desires two things only – bread and circus games." British author George Orwell expressed a similar sentiment in "1984" his novel about a dystopian future, "The people will not revolt. They will not look up from their screens long enough to notice anything has happened." He wrote that in 1949.

179. Marcus Tullius Cicero was a Roman statesman, scholar, philosopher, Academic Skeptic and attorney. He predated Juvenal by over a century but noticed the same predilections of the Roman populace even then. Bread and circuses can be effectively implemented for a very long time.

180. Human hungers are far more varied and relentless than simply one's stomach and the desire to forget one's woes.

181. The obvious counterpart to the competitive fencing callout of "touche!" – "touch!" Used in triumph and with great effect by the character Sheldon in the popular CBS sitcom, "The Big Bang Theory."

182. Meaning, "beautiful gesture," is perhaps most remembered by the movie version starring Gary Cooper in 1939. It has been remade numerous times, notably in a comedic satire by Director/Writer/Actor, Marty Feldman called, "The Last Remake of Beau Geste." I'm sure it will be remade… again.

what....?

183. Recall depends largely on repetition. That's why you're seeing another note on TOMA. Just making sure you could recall it for later use in a marketing presentation.

184. Caused by or associated with excessive secretion of hormones. (see: puberty)

185. This tidbit of wisdom is a line from "M.I.B. 3" ("Men in Black 3") and is said by the Young Agent K.

186. Cool Whip is a registered trademark of Kraft Heinz. An ingredient in Cool Whip, sodium caseinate is also used to make glue. I guess that'll really stick to your ribs.

187. Formed with or characterized by the evolution of heat, i.e.: gives off heat. Who knew heat evolved?

188. Not to be confused with the elation that comes with installing fence posts. It means to assert or assume the existence of truth. "Although I can't see it, I must postulate that you have a brain," said the student to the Philosophy 101 professor. In this case the postulation presupposes that it's not going too well and/or the rest of the semester will go downhill from there.

189. This Yiddish term refers to the one upon whom the soup is spilled. Not to be confused with "Schlemiel," which is the one who spilled the soup. These terms are more commonly recognized from the opening of "Laverne and Shirley," the 70's sitcom spinoff of "Happy Days" when the lead characters chant the hopscotch song, "Schlemiel, Schlemozzel, Hasenpfeffer, Incorporated." Hasenpfeffer is a savory rabbit stew.

190. A less than bright person who is easily duped, a pigeon, a mark. Not to be confused with the super tasty, Florida game fish known as a Snook.

191. Emotional Intelligence is gaining dominance over I.Q. in H.R. circles. While I.Q. (Intelligence Quotient) is still in common use to evaluate intelligence, it has recently been

what...?

called into question for purposes of predicting efficacy in a social work environment. Emotional Intelligence has a more accurate predictive value in this application.

192. A novel by Oscar Wilde where the main character, Dorian Gray makes a deal with the devil that he won't grow older and will live forever while a portrait of him up in the attic ages in his stead. All is good until someone sees the picture and the deal crumbles to dust, but not before revealing the horrific effects of all his sins during his extended lifetime. Owee!

193. Samuel Langhorne Clemens got the name, "Mark Twain", from his time working on a river boat. "Mark twain!" was the cry of the man on the bow keeping track of the depth of the river and would call out the reading on a regular basis. It means the depth has reached the second mark on the line at a depth of two fathoms, or 12 feet. Mark Twain was born on the apparition of Haley's Comet in 1835 and died on its cyclical reappearance, 75 years later.

194. Viktor Frankl, Sigmund Freud and Carl Jung are considered the "Fathers of Modern Psychoanalysis." Viktor was a survivor of the Concentration Camps in Nazi Germany and became the founder of Logotherapy. No, this is not the process of designing logos to feel better. It describes a search for a life meaning as the central human motivational force. It is part of existential and humanistic theoretical psychology.

195. The necessity to respond to the most important issue at the moment, in a wholly reactive mode. It precludes the application of planned action.

196. "Seize the obvious," in Latin. Really. I didn't make that up...

197. Made famous in "Bill and Ted's Excellent Adventure," and innumerable other, mindless 80's right of passage flicks.

198. The list was first compiled by Pope Gregory I somewhere

what...?

around the year 60 C.E. It included: pride, greed, lust, wrath, gluttony, envy and sloth. Conversely, he compiled a list of the Seven Virtues including: faith, hope, charity, justice, prudence, temperance and fortitude. Walt Disney came up with seven alternatives, but they were dwarfed by comparison.

199. Co-dependence is distinctly differentiated from inter-dependence, independence and dependence. Inter-dependence is similar to a symbiotic relationship where both parties benefit from the existence of the other, but without developing an existential need for the other. Independence is to stand on one's own. Dependence means to necessarily need the existence of the other party to varying degrees, up to and including existential.

200. A psychological condition where hostages develop a sympathetic bond with their captors which is irrational and dangerous for the captive. This condition was first noted in a botched bank robbery in Stockholm Sweden where hostages were held captive in a bank vault for 6 days in 1973. During the tense standoff, an obviously incongruous bond developed between the captives and the captors. Subsequently, the most famous example was when Patty Hearst, heiress to the Hearst Publishing empire was taken captive by the Symbionese Liberation Army in 1975. Ten weeks later, Hearst helped her captors rob a California bank. The list goes on and on. The syndrome has been extensively studied ever since it was first identified.

201. The behavior of the co-dependent partner to protect the addict from the effects of their addiction and facilitate the continuation of the addiction as a means of pacification and control.

202. If you've ever worked on a dairy farm, you know the day's work is not done until every one of the cows has come in to the barn, been milked and put up for the night. Generally, the cows all come home of their own accord. If they don't, something may be wrong, and the missing cow must be found and brought in.

what...?

203. Alcoholics Anonymous has changed the lives of innumerable alcoholics and those who love them.

204. A small card with the alcoholic's name on it that is given in recognition of being sober for 7 straight days.

205. A small token in either plastic or metal that is given to the alcoholic in recognition of being sober for an entire month. This becomes a keepsake for the alcoholic to keep in their pocket or with them all the time. It is a touchstone with sobriety.

206. This is a highly coveted coin, as it represents being sober for an entire year and successfully working "'The 12 Steps" along the way. It is not tied directly to the steps, but relates specifically to the amount of time being sober and having embarked on a new life – of freedom.

207. This refers to "The 12 Steps" to sobriety. It is a progressive self-revelation of the alcoholics condition and a path to recovery.

208. Step 2 involves turning to a Higher Power. No requirements are placed on which Higher Power the alcoholic chooses. It could be the universe, nature, any religion, humanity or even AA itself. To learn more about the 12 Steps, find a meeting, somewhere, anywhere or look it up online. The first step is the hardest.

209. Etymology leads us back to the Greek "keleuthos," or path. An acolyte follows the path of the leader, good or bad.

210. "Ass-kisser." I buried it here in case children accidentally pick up the book.

211. The fictitious element from the home planet of the DC Comics Classic, "Superman." Coming in contact with this rare reminder of his past negated all of Superman's superpowers, leaving him helpless in the presences of his villainous antagonists. For me, that would be redheads. So, in the words of the legendary Roberto Duran, "¡No más!"

what...?

212. A fictitious character in the "Wizard of Oz" series adapted for the movies and featuring Judy Garland in1939. The part became a classic because of the portrayal of Margaret Hamilton, who until the day she retired from the theater, always had a publicity photo from the movie posted on the door of her dressing room.

213. H_2O (see: Penn & Teller's "Water Banning Petition")

214. Turd.

215. Elephant (see: cover and all the cartoons) Relates to an antiquated 19th century taxonomic order of mammals that includes elephants, rhinoceroses and hippopotami. It is derived from the Greek for "thick skin," which is kinda' ironic because elephants are known for having sensitive skin.

216. Comes from the idiom of waiting in the apartment below for the upstairs neighbor to get fully into bed. First one shoe drops...

217. Named after English scientist, James Prescott Joule. It is a derived unit of energy listed in the International System of Units. It is equal to the energy transferred to an object in the direction of the force's motion through a distance of 1 (one) meter. Alternately, it is known as the energy dissipated as heat when an electric current measured at one ampere passes through the resistance of 1 (one) ohm for one second.

218. A name often associated with common country folk. When placed in conjunction with "Joules," presents an esoteric pun on the name of "Jules Verne," a 19th century French novelist, poet and playwright. (I guess it's really not funny if you have to explain it. However, in my defense, that was only two-thirds of a pun; "PU")

219. *sigh* More French... It just means, "And here it is."

220. These poison-resistant, genetically mutated rodents grow to extraordinary size and only the fittest survive to pass on

what...?

their hyper-adaptive and pesticide resistant genes to their prolific progeny. They can literally become as big as cats. Traditional control strategies only serve to improve the breed.

221. Fart. (see: Marie Antoinette)

222. Improvised Explosive Device. Used most effectively in asymmetrical warfare against developed countries. Low-tech is what's needed to defeat High-tech. And vice versa. Rock/Paper/Scissors. (see: Gorin No Sho)

223. High Mobility Multipurpose Wheeled Vehicle (HMMWV – the military LOVES acronyms) The first one rolled off the AM General production line in 1985.

224. A type of nuclear fusion characterized by the release of massive amount of energy, heat and radiation. (see: H-bomb)

225. A concise treatise serving to distill the essence of a large or complex work or concept.

226. A dimensionless quantity defined as a ratio of the density of a specified substance in relation to the density of water at a specified temperature.

227. The element listed in 82nd position on the Periodic Table and consists of 82 protons and 82 electrons. Pretty dense and heavy stuff.

228. The element listed in the 118th position on the Periodic Table. Reputedly the "heaviest" of all elements. You wouldn't want to drop a bunch of it on your foot.

229. No, this is not a small religious booklet designed specifically for general enlisted personnel. It stands for Gastrointestinal tract, the alimentary canal, the route from your mouth to the back door.

230. Relating to the preparation and consumption of (preferably) delicious food.

what...?

231. Honeybees live in a highly structured, social order. At the top is the Queen Bee (of which there can only be one,) a few hundred drones (all male,) and thousands of worker bees (all female, go figure.) Guess who does all the work? Guess who gets all the credit?

232. The term originated in the Hindu religion where cows are considered sacred by many of the adherents to the religion. It is based on the belief in the divine bovine-goddess, Kamadhenu. She is reputed to be the miraculous "Cow of Plenty" and can bestow whatever her owner wishes in addition to being the mother of all cattle. In India, these sacred cows are shown great deference, respect and often worship in hopes of culling benefit, irrespective of the damage and loss left in their wake.

233. It is Petruchio's assertion of unique creativity in preface to the strong-willed Kate's pun turning the phrase back on him. In Shakespeare's "Taming of the Shrew," Act 2: Scene 1, Kate responds with, "A witty mother, else her son," which in the 1600's meant that his mother had loose morals and that Petruchio was an illegitimate progeny. It was a big hit with the Groundlings in the Swan.

234. This mathematical technique is a multiple probability simulation making it possible to estimate the probable outcome(s) of an uncertain event. Its real application has only recently become viable with the advent of quantum computing which enables the massive probability calculations necessary for accurate prediction. Monte Carlo is a world renowned casino and principality on the French Riviera.

235. Third. The order goes: primary, secondary, tertiary, quaternary, quinary, senary, septenary, octonary, nonary, denary. Words also exist for twelfth order (duodenary) and twentieth order (vigenary). For the botched order, you will have to go to the drive-thru.

236. A collection of documents in chronological order designed to

what...?

demonstrate the path and development of an issue or event.

237. "Cover Your Assets" (or something like that...)

238. The final and overwhelming option generally resulting in total destruction.

239. The name of the most famous of all the quiz shows embroiled in the 50's quiz show scandals. Contestants would answer increasingly difficult questions to win a doubling amount of cash, culminating in "The $64,000 Question." The exposure of rigged shows in which contestants were given the answers and the scandal that ensued established the need for regulation and monitoring of these exceptionally popular and profitable shows for the networks.

240. A person who is in their 90's. Octogenarian is in their 80's, Septuagenarian in their 70s', Sextogenarian is in their 60's. (Sounds like fun! Perhaps that's why an unnamed retirement community in Central Florida is the STD Capital of the Southeast.)

241. Claude Denson Pepper was a left-liberal Democrat in the Florida Legislature and represented Florida in the U.S. Senate and U.S. House of Representatives ranging from 1936 to 1989. Famous for being a spokesman for Elder Rights.

242. Modern for "firm land." Part of the Italian mainland ruled by Venice during the 1600's. Not surprising in its importance to Venice considering that Venice is built on a series of pylons and manmade canals over water. Basements were in high demand and scarce supply in Venice, but their impracticality only heightened the value of terra firma. Location. Location. Location.

243. The path that an object with mass in motion will travel through space as a function of time. In classical mechanics, a trajectory is specifically determined using Hamiltonian

what...?

mechanics via canonical coordinates. According to this theorem, a complete trajectory is defined by position and momentum, simultaneously. However, according to Heisenberg's Uncertainty Principle, you can't know where you are and where you're going at the same time. In layman's language this leads one to implementation of the "Fudge Factor." Heraclitus said it more simply, "A man cannot step into the same river twice. For it's not the same river and he's not the same man." Life's a moving target. By the time you get there, the target has moved. (see: Coriolus Effect)

244. This style of writing was made popular by the French novelist, critic and essayist, Valentin Louis Georges Eugene Marcel Proust (can you imagine his mother getting really angry with him and calling him by his full name? Imagine if he had siblings and in her fury, Mom ran through the entire litany of children before she got to him. By the time she got there, she would have forgotten what she was upset about in the first place. [see: Coriolis Effect]) His most famous and monumental example of this style of writing was debuted in "A Recherche du Temps Perdu" ("Remembrance of Things Past" or "In Search of Lost Time") in seven volumes from 1913 to 1927. Try as one might, not even Evelyn Wood is going to be able to read it in one sitting.

245. This is a nod to the 1999 sci-fi action film, "The Matrix" during which Morpheus (Lawrence Fishburne) offers the choice to Neo (Keanu Reeves) between maintaining the status quo and remaining in contented ignorance or going forward in the uncertainty of the real world, as signified by the choice between taking the red pill or the blue pill. The red pill is life changing. The blue pill is the status quo.

246. Kool-Aid is a registered trademark of Kraft General Foods since 1953. Between 1955 and 1978, the Rev. Jim ones led a cult that culminated in their mass-murder/suicide in "Jonestown," Guyana on Nov. 18, 1978, by drinking Kool-Aid laced with every poison he could lay his hands on. The Kool-Aid brand had nothing to do with the incident.

what...?

247. The recent onset of puberty and all the madness that it entails.

248. In the animal kingdom, especially in herd or pack animals, there is an on-going conflict to establish superiority among dominant males. The goal is to be the "Alpha" or "First" among all other challengers. This is especially evident during rutting season and any Friday night in a Honky-Tonk.

249. To be held motionless either by fear/amazement/awe, or simply impaled on a pointed implement. Given the choice, I prefer the former.

250. From the Latin meaning, "the existing state of affairs." Not to be confused with Nevada.

251. Also "Tunnels" and "Plugs." These are the devices forced in ever increasing sizes into holes in various parts of the anatomy. They are thought to make one more attractive. (see: Ubangi)

252. From the French, "Advance Guard." This generally refers to the people or the works that they bring forth that are radical, experimental or unorthodox in respect to the status quo. Initially they tend to be resisted, but become more acceptable with the passage of time and proliferation of use primarily in the cultural realm. It's also the name of a typeface that ironically is now classic, standard and commonplace. Funny thing about clichés; originally they were fresh and unique, then became tired and worn through overuse. (see: your High School graduation picture) P.S. Your Man-Bun will look as ridiculous to you as my Mullet does to me in the years to come...

253. A person in the early 60's who strove for self-expression by rejecting the mores and superficial aspects of conventional society. Based on the "Beat Generation" literary movement of the late '40's to mid-'50's, they did not aspire to change society to their norms, but to simply reject it and create their own counter-culture. Maynard G. Krebs was the poster child.

what...?

254. *A person during the late 60's and early 70's who strove for self-expression by rejecting the mores and superficial aspects of conventional society (including Beatniks). Based on a youth movement advocating drugs and free-love, it spread worldwide. They did not aspire to change society to their norms, but to simply reject it and create their own counter-culture. (sound familiar?) Woodstock was the defining event of the era. Anyone who remembers the '60's wasn't there... (see: tie-dyed)*

255. *A person in the early 21st century who strove for self-expression by rejecting the mores and superficial aspects of conventional society. While claiming to be authentic and unique, they are ironically and universally recognized as lacking in authenticity and uniqueness in their desire for total conformity to their collective style. They did not aspire to change society to their norms, but to simply reject it and create their own counter-culture. (Do you hear an echo in here...?) (see: consumption geared toward commodification of rebellion or counter-culture)*

256. *The Wall Street Journal.*

257. *A Freudian psychoanalytical construct describing the attribution of one's own failings on another in order to avoid assuming accountability for one's own actions. The flip-side of this construct is unforgiveness, which is where you take the poison and wait for the other person to die.*

258. *Regarded as sacred and inviolable. A combination of the words, "sacred" and "sanctified." (set apart solely for holy use)*

259. *Not to be confused with climbing in the saddle on your horse named "Tanta." It simply means, "equivalent."*

260. *Elvis' manager.*

261. *Reputedly the best actor ever with the only real competition coming from the theatrical side in the person*

what...?

of Sir Lawrence Olivier in terms of esteem. His 60 year career garnered him 2 Oscars for Best Actor, 3 BAFTA Awards for Best Foreign Actor and 2 Golden Globes for Best Actor. He is best remembered for his portrayal of Don Vito Corleone in "The Godfather."

262. "New York, New York, so good you have to say it twice." And so I did (see: #62)

263. Also known as the "Benefit-Cost Ratio" is another project management term communicating the profitability indicator used in cost-benefit analysis. "Is what you spent on the project worth what you got out of it?"

264. This is a bit of a trick question. His true rookie card was in 1914 in the minor leagues and was only available in red and blue. It recently sold for around $6M. His Major League "rookie" card with the yellow background recently went for well north of $500K.

265. This phrase is from the 1939 "Wizard of Oz" in the opening Emerald City scenes. The carriage was drawn by a horse that intermittently changed color from white to red to yellow to purple. Prior to CG, this was accomplished with the use of four different horses that had lemon, grape and cherry gelatin powder on them. Takes had to be quick in order to film the horses before they sweated or licked off the sweet powder.

266. All lifeforms that we know of are carbon-based. Only sci-fi has proffered the concept of silicon-based lifeforms, or more exotic energy-based life forms. Frankly, I'm kinda' partial to the carbon-based ones.

267. Plant life and animal life.

268. This effect is used to explain the interconnectedness of all life on earth and by extension, the universe. It posits that if a butterfly flaps its wings in the Amazon rainforest, the cascading effect will over the course of time affect every

what...?

molecule on the planet. No action is without consequences. (So, how is it they can time travel in the movies and be convinced they won't "change anything" as long as they don't affect the outcome of the focal event?) "If a man speaks in the forest and there's no woman to hear him, is he still wrong?"

269. Military term for maintaining active scanning and relentless alertness.

270. This is a great tool for assessing the potential impact of conditions on a project or initiative. It allows the viewer to visualize both the positive and negative risks inherent in the situation. Not to be confused with SWAT (Special Weapons and Tactics.) Confusing the two can lead to much bigger problems.

271. Lego is a registered trademark of The Lego Group. They have had an interesting road trying to protect their trademark, In 2000 they trademarked the 3-dimensional brick when the 2-dimensional trademark registration expired in 1998 after having been originally trademarked in 1973. The 3-dimensional logo of the brick was the first of its kind to be trademarked. The claim has subsequently been successfully challenged in 2015 in the U.S. Meanwhile, it hasn't stopped anybody from playing with them.

272. If anyone ever says to you, "The money's not the point, it's the principle of the thing," know in your heart of hearts, it's the money...

273. This means it's capable of continuing or renewing itself/oneself indefinitely. Once sought unicornistically by inventors the world over in the form of a perpetual motion machine. But then, there's that pesky entropy again. However, ironically enough, there are a few notable exceptions. (see; politicians or the mildew on your shower curtain)

274. Overly bright colors, exceedingly ornamented and especially in a vulgar or tasteless way (see: Mardi Gras)

what...?

275. *Ostentatiously or tastelessly over-ornamented. Coincidentally, (or not) the artist and architect Antoni Gaudi epitomized the word in his work. His creations were impressively grand and often asymmetrical in design, incorporating bright colors, non-traditional materials and construction techniques. He incorporated a very organic feel in his breathtaking designs that are considered national treasures in Spain. And rightly so.*

276. *Lacking in the social graces. Translated from the French it means, "left."(see: Rive Gauche, "left bank")*

277. *A puzzling, unsolved or difficult problem. i.e.: "Why do we park on a driveway and drive on a parkway?"*

278. *Kenjutsu is the art of active combat with the sword, in this case the katana, or killing sword of Japanese legend. There are no "do-overs" in this regard. The loser is dead and the winner goes on to another "contest." It is a book that very comprehensively communicates the timeless principles of mortal struggle and mastery over the conflict that undergirds every level of human interaction. It's about winning. Period.*

279. *Undeniably the most famous and skilled of all samurai, Musashi epitomized the extreme focus and preparation necessary for successful "strategy," by his definition, "the means of defeating one's opponent." Conversely, the Western mindset developed a totally different methodology for strategy.*

   NUGGET ALERT! *It can be simply stated as GOST (Goal/Objectives/Strategies/Tactics) It is a simple hierarchy for creating a comprehensive plan to succeed, whether it is in a military campaign or a marketing/advertising campaign. It is flexible in application but remains rigid in architecture. Simply put: "Follow the plan. Modify the details."*

   For every endeavor, there can only be one overarching goal, not multiple. It is always achieved passively. To accomplish the singular goal, a select group of objectives must be

what...?

actively achieved. Once they are achieved, the goal will have been accomplished - passively. Not until. Objectives are the critical mass of the goal. Nothing more. Nothing less.

Various methodologies for achieving specific objectives are called, "strategies." A strategy may support more than one objective. Each objective may have numerous strategies. But, a strategy must support at least one objective. If it does not support at least one objective, it must necessarily be eliminated.

Tactics are all dictated by strategies. NOT the other way around. They are the means to implement the strategies. Again, if the tactic doesn't support a strategy, it must be eliminated, immediately. People tend to drop to the tactical level first as a way to approach a campaign. That is a mission-critical error.

If you simply follow this GOST hierarchy relentlessly and consistently, your chances of success are dramatically enhanced. Combining the "Book of Five Rings" and GOST results in a reflexively Agile approach to changing conditions, executed within a consistent framework for prioritized decision making, resulting in the highest probability of success in the endeavor.

Not to be confused with "Ghost in the Machine," which is an existential philosophy that defines human consciousness and thought as a separate and distinct entity from the corporeal body. By extension, virtual consciousness (artificial sentience?) is thought to result from artificial intelligence inside a computer. I'll let the philosophers and digital ethicists work that one out...

280. The seminal work of cross-cultural situational awareness, "Left of Bang," published by Black Irish Entertainment LLC, outlines the skills necessary to survive in a hostile environment, in any culture. It is on the Marine Corps Commandant's Professional Reading List.

what...?

281. Patrick Van Horne and Jason A. Riley are the co-authors of "Left of Bang." Both are Marines (There's no such thing as a former-Marine.) Oorah!

282. The favorite expression of amazement by Inspector Gadget, the cartoon hero of the media franchise of the same name ("So, why didn't he say, 'eponymous' this time?") [Ed. Note: "Go figure."]

283. Sounds very Shakespearian, but it's not. It is attributed to an early 19th century Scottish author, Sir Walter Scott from his epic poem, "Marmion: A Tale of Flodden Field." Now aren't you glad you asked? Hmmmm…?

284. A wall, earthen rampart, person, institution or principle that acts as a main defense against attack. It comes from the Middle English, or Middle Dutch (bolwerk or bolwerc), or Middle Low German (bollwerk,) meaning bole (tree trunk) and work. Stable, strong and unrelenting in its defense. Strong as garlic.

285. Crocs is a registered trademark of Crocs, Inc. Considered gauche by hipsters and other cool kids. I find the combination very comfortable and couldn't care less what other people think about my choice of sartorial pedal accoutrement.

286. French entomologist, August Magnan noted in the 1930's that the insect's flight was actually impossible. It became "common knowledge," until 2005 when Michael Dickenson, a professor of biology and insect flight expert at the University of Washington published his study in the journal Proceedings of the National Academy of Sciences. He proved through the use of high-speed photography and force sensors on larger-than-life robotic bees flapping in mineral oil that the bee flaps its wings forward and backward, not up and down. According to his description, "more like a crappy helicopter propeller." The turbulence beneath the wings is lower pressure than the air above the wings, which allows them to stay aloft.

what...?

287. Tell that to Tom Brady...

288. Humiliated, as in bluffed out of a big pot in poker.

289. From the Sanskrit, "kamma." Believed in Hinduism and Buddhism as a means to perpetuate transmigration (from one life to the next via reincarnation) and in its ethical consequences to determine the general or specific nature of one's next existence. Put simply, "what goes around, comes around."

290. A scientific concept and measurable physical property most commonly associated with a state of disorder, randomness and uncertainty. (see: a teenager's room between visits by parents.) Also known as the 2nd Law of Classical Thermodynamics.

291. Technically, there are 4 Laws of Thermodynamics but they have a very strange numbering: Zeroth, First, Second and Third. Ralph H. Fowler discovered the Zeroth Law in 1935 and defined it as thermal equilibrium. But, already there were so many books published with the 1st, 2nd and 3rd laws that he was forced to adopt the number "zero." A discussion of the Four Laws could fill a book by itself (and has, on numerous occasions.)

292. Certainly one of my favorite laws of physics. When I obey it, I don't bump into stuff which creates fewer bruises and keeps my wife happy around her antiques.

293. Automatic Teller Machines made their debut on Sept. 2, 1969 at Chemical Bank in Rockville Centre, New York. We have been addicted to them ever since. As cash disappears, so will they.

294. Intuitively, these appear to derive from the specific marks of standard on a craftsman's workbench. However, they are actually land surveyor's designations, often related to iron stakes or L-shaped posts driven into the ground back in the day when surveying was done with links and chains.

what...?

295. A relatively recent (as of the early 70's) horse racing term regarding a bet whereby the bettor correctly picks the First, Second and Third place finishers of a race in the proper order. It has since been adopted by any number of disciplines whereby the selection of three specific items is made correctly, especially if the odds are significantly against winning the bet.

296. Originally from the Latin, "solidus," referring to a Roman gold coin meaning "coin of thick or solid metal" not of thin plate. In the absence of gold coins out in the far reaches of the empire, the soldiers were often paid in salt, hence the word "salary." In this case, men who were paid in salt to fight for the Emperor. Hence the term, "He's worth his salt."

297. Often called "the Ultimate Grillers' Steak" because of its well-marbleized meat, tender texture and succulent flavor. Sign me up!

298. Undeniably my favorite method of grilling steak. Start by getting the grill literally red hot and momentarily searing both sides of the steak to seal in the juices, then immediately switch to a medium low flame to cook the steak to your desired doneness. Let the steak sit and rest on the plate for a moment to let the juices do their thing and then serve with a side of kvelling.

299. Oh, golly… French again. Meaning a display or feat of strength, ingenuity or skill.

300. The act of committing a specific motor task to physiological memory through repetition. Especially valuable for reactive responses and when the athlete is in bonk and can't think straight.

301. This is a term used by middle managers to bludgeon their subordinates while appearing to be acting in the best interests of "the company." Initially, it was a beneficial process to identify and document the best and most efficient ways to accomplish a task for the purpose of process

what...?

improvement. It was quickly overtaken by personal agendas. Instead, may I suggest the Japanese discipline of Kaizen – the process of constant and incremental improvement. Once you have established a "best practice," it is already obsolete.

302. A lofty, extravagantly colorful, bombastic and playfully pompous style.

303. The use of excessive language to obfuscate the point and/or "beat around the bush." "If you can't dazzle them with brilliance, baffle them with bull-puckey."

304. An adage or tersely phrased statement of truth. A proverb.

305. Referring to the suits (hearts, spades, diamonds and clubs) in a deck of playing cards. To be heavy in a particular suit. Not to be confused with a "Big 'n Tall" men's haberdashery or particularly verbose legal torts.

306. Adverb referring to the use of multiple meanings for the same word or phrase. Generally used to mislead. Equivocation is one of the classical logical fallacies used with great aplomb by politicians and late-nite infomercials.

307. A fictional character created by J.R.R. Tolkien and successfully used to spread joy and fantasy throughout the childhoods (and adulthoods) of audiences since 1937. They are imaginary people about half the height of humans, but with all the flaws and peccadilloes. They have over-sized feet with broad, leathery soles with curly hair on top, inclining them to go barefoot throughout life. They live in comfy, little cottages in the ground, generally hillsides with small windows that look out over the beautiful countryside. The book and subsequent series was started unintentionally by Tolkein while he was in the midst of grading essays in 1930. He simply wrote the classic opening line, "In a hole in the ground there lived a hobbit." The rest is Middle Earth history.

308. The base of operations for the Hobbits. Most notably: Bilbo

what...?

Baggins, Frodo Baggins, Samwise Gamgee, Meriadoc Brandybuck and Peregrin Took. Gollum took other lodgings.

309. *Sam's favorite. Perhaps the start of the "All Day Breakfast" phenomena to capture the imaginations of restauranteurs the world over. A quaint habit of having an additional repast before lunch.*

310. *Originating as a mark used in Great Britain to denote established standards of quality and purity in precious metals. Not to be confused with expensive, syrupy greeting cards and terminally romantic chic flics.*

311. *To advocate for, or adhere to in strong deference. (e.g.: "Yes, dear.") From the word "Spouse." You do the math.*

312. *A connoisseur or someone with unusually specialized or superior skills in a subject or refined taste. Generally referred to in the plural. (see: people who really need to think they are better than everybody else.)*

313. *To beget or procreate. To give rise to an emotion, opinion or action.*

314. *Extending or existing beyond the limits of ordinary experience. Other than. Separate and distinct from, but inextricably linked to. (see: an unflickable booger.)*

315. *Literally, "ten thousand." Or in ancient common usage, an uncountable number.*

316. *Noun; a collective, clustered in a dense mass, Verb; to gather together as in a mixture of components able to be separated by mechanical means ("He really needs to aggregate his excremental material.")*

317. *An intransitive verb meaning to speak or write about something in an overtly praising or boastful way. To break one's arm while patting oneself on the back.*

318. *I made that one up. Everything sounds so cool and official*

what...?

when you put it in Latin. It means, "I live therefore I am creative." My Latin teacher in high school would be so proud of me, especially now that I'm a founding member of the Consortium Flatae Venerati ("Old Fart's Club.")

319. Permanent, like a Sharpie (Sharpie is a registered trademark of Newell Brands) on your brand new, sparkling white tuxedo shirt right before you walk down the aisle, or everything you say on the internet.

320. Capturing attention as if by a magic spell, fascinatingly attractive, excruciatingly attractive. Kinda' like my wife Keiko on that first group bike ride. P.S. It kinda' went both ways. She saw me in Spandex, and had to have me. (Currently, Spandex is a registered trademark of a German dental appliance company Hager & Werken who make "Cheek and lip expanders for dental surgical purposes." You can't make this stuff up.) You can ask Keiko if you don't believe me. Personally, I think a license should be required to wear it in public...

321. Generally, a short-lived, intensely fixated and unreasoned passion for a person or thing. It can only be accurately assessed in retrospect. (Oh, great... Thanks.) Mostly experienced by the young, but when experienced by older and supposedly wiser people it results in exponentially greater embarrassment for everyone directly or indirectly involved. ("The only thing worse than a fool, is an old fool.")

322. Not to be confused with a brand of electronics, this is the peak of an arc or trajectory, the highest point. The converse is the nadir and refers to the point of the celestial sphere that is diametrically opposed to the zenith. (Not to be confused with Ralph who put the last nail in the coffin of the Corvair.)

323. Falling off directly as in, "off the face of a vertical cliff," or rain falling from the sky (precipitation.) Not to be confused with the anticipation associated with that first sip of an ice cold, adult beverage after mowing the lawn in 90 degree heat.

what...?

324. Adjective relating to great destruction or total annihilation. (see: "Nothing parties like a rental.")

325. To cause to continue, or increase numerically by sexual or asexual reproduction. Intentionally distributed. To spread throughout a network as in from one hub or backbone to another on the internet. From the British, to enter through the correct entrance in the fence, "Ey, Mate. Make sure you go in fru' da propagate."

326. Capable of being discerned by one or more of the tactile senses, palpable, material or substantial. Not to be confused with having the ability to be made to taste like a tangerine. (see: Skittles [Skittles is a registered trademark of Mars Inc.'s Wrigley Unit])

327. Having the power to spread throughout, having a pervading quality. (see: S.B.D. "Silent, but deadly.")

328. See page 100.

329. Netflix is a registered trademark of Netflix, Inc. and has provided an inexhaustible plethora of bingeworthy entertainment during "The Great Quarantine." WFH just wouldn't be the same without it.

330. Synonymous with "accountability" in marketing/advertising.

331. Benjamin Franklin was one of the founding fathers of the United States of America. As such, his wisdom pervades much of the Declaration of Independence as well as the founding principles and documents of our Nation. Having an extraordinarily broad and comprehensive knowledge of a wide range of subjects, he became known as a polymath, a term coined by philosopher Johann von Werwen in Hamburg in 1603.

332. Difficult, if not impossible to restrain or control. (see: bad hair day or boys carrying their books in front of them in middle school)

what...?

333. *Earthshaking, pertaining to an earthquake or other seismological event, Tektonic plate movement. "Honey, did you feel the earth move?"*

334. *The pinnacle of Maslow's Hierarchy of Needs. While this seems to be an attainable goal in writing, it should be considered more of an empirical absolute to which we can aspire. It calls to us continually, but perfection is always just out of reach. That doesn't mean we shouldn't strive for it. On the contrary. It can be your North Star or total realization of your creative genius.*

335. *The ability to be shaped by the strike of a hammer or pressure, as in a roller. From the Latin "malleus" for hammer. Also the small bone that transfers vibration to the incus in conjunction with the stapes (stirrup) which facilitates the perception of sound in the human middle ear.*

336. *Barbie is a registered trademark of Mattel, Inc. and was born on March 15, 1959 at the American International Toy Fair in New York. She was created by Ruth Handler, a wife of one of the founders of Mattel as a way to diverge from the ubiquitous baby dolls of the era and give young girls the sense that they could be anything they wanted to be. The doll was named after her daughter.*

337. *Matchbox is the registered trademark of Mattel, Inc. The original die-cast metal toy cars were made by the Lesney Co. (A mixture of the names of the originators; Leslie Smith and Rodney Smith, no relation) in 1947. They have since become a favorite and formative toy for children around the world and is challenged only by Lego blocks as the premier midnight, barefoot, household landmine of all time.*

338. *Those ginormous, pick up trucks with the four huge, side-by-side wheels in the back.*

339. *Ernest Miller Hemingway was perhaps the greatest American novelist and short-story writer. Having won the Nobel prize for literature, he described his succinct and lucid*

what...?

prose style as befitting the "iceberg theory." He understood brokenness all too well and succumbed to it at the age of 61 by his own hand. A tragic loss on so many levels.

340. A patriotic nod to the framers of the Declaration of Independence who consciously chose to use the less popular spelling of "inalienable" to draw attention to itself. It is not a typo in either case.

341. A feeling of insecurity, anxiety or apprehension. Also, the abbreviation for "Ångstrom," an obsolete unit of measurement that was used to measure the distance between sub-atomic particles. It is one ten-billionth of a metre. Wow, talk about sweating the small stuff... Sheesh.

342. Developers that are entirely too smart for their own good and have too much time on their hands will often embed small, subprograms in software to be found by the cognoscenti. One of the most famous of which was "The Hall of Tortured Souls" to be found in the 1995 iteration of Microsoft Excel (Microsoft and Excel are registered trademarks of Microsoft Corp.) It features the name of the developers on the project and even shows their pictures in a game-type environment. By traversing numerous elevated pathways you can enter various rooms. I wonder how these developers like working in Siberia now...

343. Not straightforward or candid, calculating, insincere or feigning naiveté. Playing "dumb."

344. To pass on or delegate to another, to cause to roll onward and downward, and to all those who have proudly served our country in the military, we all know which direction poopie goes...

345. Messin' around with words to avoid directly dealing with the subject.

346. The use of psychological or psychiatric-sounding jargon to obfuscate the meaning intended. To hide the fact that they

what...?

have no clue what they're talking about, but want to sound like they really do. High-falutin' shrink talk. Not to be confused with the mindless ramblings of a serial killer on death row. But, then again...

347. Difficult to understand or interpret, impenetrable to inquiry or investigation.

348. Intricate or complicated. Having numerous overlapping folds, like the surface of a brain. Twisted asymmetrically. Getting directions on your phone that always seem to want to route you through Milwaukee, regardless of where you begin. (P.S. Just for fun sometime, ask your phone to give you directions to Buckingham Palace. It's quite amusing, actually.)

349. The representation of abstract principles or ideas in a dramatic, narrative or pictorial form. To describe something in ways that do not in any way relate to the true meaning or intention of the words or phrases (see: allegorical interpretation as proposed by Origen in the early 4th century.) Once you have cut the mooring, you can take the boat wherever you want.

350. An indirect reference to something. Not to be confused with "illusion" which is often created or supported by misdirection of attention to mask the actual action or intent (see: magic or poli-sci)

351. Existing or happening during the same period of time, generally currently in the moment.

352. Intended to be understood only by a small and/or specialized group. (see: cognoscenti or teenagers on social media.)

353. In a high degree; conspicuously and with authority of presence and substantive foundation. You can always walk through a door that says, "No Admittance," as long as you act like you're supposed to be there. However, staying there is another matter.

what...?

354. *Refers to a simulation of true random pattern. A true random pattern is an absolute, and as such can never be empirically achieved. It can only be simulated or consist of a pattern that is larger than the perception or comprehension of the intended audience. (i.e.: If the historical record cannot substantiate the evolution of a specific lifeform, simply put its beginning beyond the comprehension of the audience in hundreds of billions of years or time frames of a higher order of magnitude.) The Japanese developed a method of fine art printing called rotogravure, that simulated the grain of film but was mechanically produced to create the illusion of seamlessly fine gradients of color. With the advent of large format printers, raster image processors would scatter the printed dots in such a way as to reduce the banding or rosettes found in traditional four-color process printing. If you look r-e-e-e-a-a-a-l-l-y close at the cover of this book, you will see the little patterns I'm talking about. They consist of four colors of ink (cyan/magenta/yellow/black – CMYK) and by proximity and density create the illusion of a wide array of colors. Your eye does the rest. Stochastic screens simply do it better.*

355. *Richard was the owner and manager of the Steinmetz Home for Wayward Boys. He is retired now, but was a consummate professional photographer that I often referred to as, "Sure Shot," because he always got the shot I needed somewhere in the course of our photo shoots. Richard taught me much over the course of our 37+ year friendship, not the least of which was how to throw a wildly successful party for 37 Japanese Odaiko drummers (that didn't speak a word of English) in his backyard, on the Fourth of July. But, that's another story. I have many.*

bios...

steve buck

author, teacher, friend, obvious kinda' guy

Mr. Buck was born at a very early age in Cincinnati, Ohio to sensible Midwestern parents who had unrealistically optimistic expectations for his future. Abandoning a free-ride *(tuition, books, room and board)* at the University of Cincinnati, he sold his MG Midget and ran away to NYC to become a rich and famous actor. After an extended, but stellar career waiting tables, he was encouraged by threat of imminent starvation to return to his design roots.

Steve lied his way into his first job in advertising and started as an Art Director at a Madison Avenue ad agency. Within a few short years he opened his own agency, Douglaston/Stevens, in the now trendy Chelsea area of Manhattan. He continued to knock around advertising after he emigrated to Tampa. But, his passion has always been teaching and writing. So, this book became the obvious venue to pursue his creativity, sleep indoors and take regular meals.

And in spite of everything, his wife still loves him.

phillip ortiz

artist, illustrator, designer, cartoonist, family man

Phillip was the obvious choice to breathe life into the characters of Schnitzl & P'Nut. He is responsible for not only creating the characters, but he has an obvious understanding of them at the molecular level.

His passion for all things creative and his delight in family has given his work a depth and relatable flair seldom seen among his contemporaries. This book represents yet another step in what will surely be a stellar career for Phillip. Keep an eye on this one. There are great things to come... obviously!

Special Thanks !

To Jerry Greenfield for being a good friend and saving me from myself as my Editor. It's good to have another old ad dog in the trenches with you, especially one who has known you for over 37 years.

To Stratton Smith for believing in me when it felt like no one else did. And especially for calling me "the Master of the Obvious." I was sincerely offended for almost an entire minute before I realized the obvious wisdom in what you said.

To Jeff & Jen Perushek for facilitating my social media epiphany and giving me all the love, support and directions to make it happen.

To Mona Burrows-Andrews for her serendipitous encouragement to finally "write a book." You are the one who ultimately pushed me into the pool.

To Stephen Fussell who saw something in me when we first met and convinced me to apply to Mensa. Miller Analogies is our friend.

To Mel Burnett, a staunch good friend and ally. A Super-Geek (with a capital "G") and chief facilitator of my digital extravaganza. I couldn't have done it without you.

And lastly, but certainly not leastly, to Keiko - the love of my life and completer of my dreams.